A Century of British Aeroplanes in Old Photographs

Arthur W. J. G. Ord-Hume

When Heston Aircraft Ltd was formed out of the old Comper Aircraft Ltd, it was a major shift of emphasis. Nicholas Comper had never been interested in running a profitable company. All he wanted to do was to enjoy designing and building ever-faster sporting light aeroplanes. Heston's board of directors, however, had different ideas. They wanted to run a profitable company come what may. All the original Comper directors, including Nickolas himself, were disposed of and the new business started off with a clean slate to design and built what by 1930s standards would be classed as an executive light aircraft. It was, of course, the elegant Heston Phoenix with its retractable undercarriage.

Stenlake Publishing Ltd

© 2022 Arthur W.J.G. Ord-Hume
First Published in the United Kingdom, 2022
Stenlake Publishing Limited
54-58 Mill Square, Catrine, KA5 6RD
www.stenlake.co.uk

Printed by
Blissetts,
Unit E1-E8 Shield Drive,
West Cross Ind Pk,
Brentford, TW8 9EX

ISBN 978-1-84033-933-8

Above: Built in July 1939 as an open two-seater, this DH.94 Moth Minor survived Impressment as AW112 to be restored and altered to a coupé model at Panshanger in 1954. *Below*: An imported airliner, a Ford 4AT-E, G-ABEF, poses with the first Comper Swifts, G-AARX (ABC Scorpion) and G-AARX (Pobjoy). *Bottom*: A Luton LA-4 Minor, G-AFIR, and a Skyways Avro York at Stansted, September 8th, 1956.

Preface

We are well into the 21st century now – a fifth of the way in fact – yet we tend still to look back on the 20th as if it was only a mere and reassuringly comfortable yesterday. Just as the last century actually began in the Victorian era – remember the venerable old Queen Victoria did not die until January 1901 – our modern age, with all its fears and foibles, not to mention the worldwide disruption created by the fearsome Covid-19 pandemic, leans heavily upon the era that presaged it. Nowhere is this more evident than in the world of aviation.

There are plenty amongst us who revel in rapidly-advancing technology and are perfectly at home with today's futuristic-looking aircraft. Even today we have difficulty in identifying one or two designs as being aircraft at all! Some jet fighters today seem at impossible variance with all we ever learned about aerodynamics, let alone structures and design. After all, in the 1920s almost every aeroplane had the recurring theme of bracing wires, propellers and open cockpits. And that included on the one hand military aircraft and on the other those used for joy-riding.

The fact is that, in the 1930s, today's modern super-fast sky-cleavers would have appeared to have emerged from outer space! Older people feel slightly uncomfortable eying an angular jet plane with its tiny wing-span and not a bracing-wire in sight! Others involuntarily sigh and shed a tear for the missing propeller, the leather flying helmet and the open cockpit.

When Scottish aviation pioneer Preston Albert Watson made his first heavier-than-air flying machine in 1903, his rocking-wing'd glider, later to be fitted with a Dutheil et Chalmers twin-cylinder engine, was *almost* a Victorian invention. This is one of the foibles of industrial history – it is hard to establish the difference between when something *first began* and when there was a 'first happening'. Those Americans, the brothers Wright, had a good PR set-up that made certain the whole world knew the date when they flew for the first time. Other pioneers, while dexterous with saw and spanner, were probably less able to remember dates and historical protocol. Because they did not expect to be creating an event that would have to take its place in history, they didn't bother to write down the date. Or even when they first had the idea!

And so their historically important dates are vague and in the 'I think it might have been last Tuesday or possibly the previous Sunday' realm. We can understand that, for in the heat of the moment, the approach to the ultimate goal may well obscure the sedulous adhesion to the pocket calendar.

Which uncovers that perennial hot-potato 'who was the first person to fly a heavier-than-air machine'! I am not going to get involved in that controversy, for the past 60 years have seen many claims and counter-claims which question Kittihawk's prominence. My good friend Charles Gibbs-Smith (1909–1981) spent many years looking into this and still, at the end, could not say with certainty. No, the weight of probability rests with those Yankee bicycle-dealers and I don't want to be the one to spoil a good story.

My real interest lies with what happened after that or, more to the point, what happened after the First World War had aged aviation into a premature maturity and flying was taken up both as a new sport and a challenge as well as commercially as a means of taking people from A to B in exchange for money. Admittedly, people didn't really appreciate all that went into this flying business and genuine dangers loomed large and real from behind friendly canvas hangar doors. And, of course, private flying, military aviation and commercial air transport were all lumped under one umbrella.

Expressed simply, and as hinted at earlier when I mentioned that all aircraft possessed 'recurring themes', this means there was little difference between private and commercial flying as distinct from Service or military flight. And if aircraft were similar, airfields were equally unsophisticated, and all pilots were trained to an equal, rather basic, standard. From the 'A' Licence to a full commercial licence was an easy task. In today's universal slang, it was no slog and but a mere doddle – whatever a 'doddle' may be!

This all sounds pretty good and well-defined until we look a little deeper into the subject and we make the dubious discovery that while it is, on the surface, easy to separate civil from military flight, in truth there is a measure of uncertainty – a sort of blurring of the join separating the two. While predominantly civil aircraft, one or two interesting military (meaning Royal Air Force) are included. These have been chosen on the grounds that they may be pertinent to the flow of my story-in-pictures. We'll find it as we go along but this is to alert you to the presence of a few anomalies.

Another problem we have to face is that I claim these to be all British aircraft, yet some are clearly not! Before you start getting hot under the collar, I'll explain that there are times when a story has to be expanded in directions which may not be expected. Consider, for a moment, the link between shop-fitters and aircraft-makers Sage of Peterborough and the American Aeronca firm, or Frenchman Roger Druine and the Rollason Turbulent. And even the familiar Auster, seen by some as being about as English as a cream tea, disrupts our very concept of something's *Britishness* when we find it can trace its origins back to America where, confusingly, an Englishman designed the first Taylorcraft. See what I mean?

What this does prepare you for is that you will find a smattering of non-British aircraft chosen for their interest or association with Britain. In general, this is a book about aircraft as distinct from helicopters and balloons, airships and autogiros – but don't be surprised if you find the odd one has got through!

In the same way, while predominantly about photographs of civil aircraft, it's not exclusively so. If there's a good picture with a valid reason for inclusion, I have put it in.

I have been taking and collecting pictures for many years and a recent trawl through my files revealed quite a number of shots that I thought were interesting and some which bordered on the 'jolly exciting' definition. In fact I thought that these might be worth a wider audience so I am sharing them with you. Some are possibly familiar, but where this presentation may differ is in what I may be able to explain about the image. Hence the occasionally very long caption!

Pictures that have not been taken by me are, wherever possible, credited to the copyright-holder where this is known. In a distressingly large number or instances, the name of the original photographer is unknown. To those unknowns whose pictures I have used, please accept my thanks and appreciation.

The front cover picture is a special one. My first love, dare I confess, was the Comper Swift and at various times I was custodian of G-ABTC and G-ABPE, aeroplanes that were the same age as me! And when my late friend, Airspeed and DH test pilot Ronald 'Ron' Edward Clear (1917-2004) took over George Errington's G-ACTF, one-time VT-ADO *Scarlet Angel*, I was in my element. That aircraft is now at the Shuttleworth Collection, Old Warden, where this picture was taken on September 7th, 2014.

Picture quality remains, as ever, an unfortunate variable. I would rather give you a poor picture of a rare event or an interesting aeroplane than leave it out altogether, so for this reason please understand that not all my pictures are of the top-most studio quality. Rotten pictures leap from the page and influence the minds of pernickety observers, not those who understand the value of a scarce event captured in an otherwise dreadful photo!

The arrangement of the photographs is loosely chronological as defined by registration. As for the selection, this is mine which means that occasionally you may ask yourself why I chose it. Well, there you have your answer. I don't think you will be too disappointed! I rest my case…

The son of an eminent barrister-at-Law who was at one time Clerk of the Crown at the High Court of Calcutta, London-born Harold Hume Piffard (1867-1938) was a true aviation pioneer. Educated at Shoreham's Lancing College, he became an accomplished artist exhibiting at the Royal Academy between 1895 and 1899, later illustrating books for boys. His studio/workshop was at 18 Addison Grove, Bedford Park, Chiswick in West London. Early in the 1900s, he began to take an interest in aviation and made several models. The first full-size machine was made in Chiswick with the aid of two carpenters and taken to a shed rented from the engineering firm set up by John Isaac Thornycroft in Turnham Green for final assembly and engine testing. In September 1909 a field was rented in North Ealing by Hanger Lane Farm: this was close to the short-lived Acton Aerodrome. The aircraft flew on December 2nd 1909 but that night it and its shed were destroyed in a gale. In the quest for more space, he then joined solicitor George Wingfield and set up The Aviators' Finance Co Ltd, leasing land next to New Salts Farm, Shoreham, as a flying field. Here he built and flew the aircraft shown here – the Piffard Biplane No.2 – on May 21st, 1910. The wing-span was 34 feet and the engine a 35hp ENV 8-cylinder Type D water-cooled motor driving a 7-ft diameter Weiss propeller.

One of the founding members of the Royal Aero Club was pioneer aviator Lieut-Col Sir Francis Kennedy McClean (1876–1955). He flew with Wilbur Wright at Le Mans and, early in 1909, began an association with the brothers Short to develop aircraft in Britain. McLean owned the ground on which the aerodromes at Leysdown and then Eastchurch were built. He held Royal Aero Club Aviators Certificate No.21 after flying a Short S.27 biplane at Eastchurch in 1910 and was to become one of the founders of naval aviation and amateur flying. Between 1909 and 1914 he owned no fewer than 16 aircraft, all but one built by Shorts. He is seen here in the front cockpit of the Short S.59, one of a variety of similar (but not identical) pusher biplanes built in the period 1912-13. This one remained Short Brothers' property for some time and was occasionally flown by Maurice Egerton (1874-1958) who later became the 4th and last baron of Tatton. McLean, a pioneer in aerial photography, went down in history when, on August 10th, 1912, he flew the Short S.33 through London's Tower Bridge.

Here is the Grahame-White Military Biplane Type V1 which was shown at Olympia in February 1913. The first aircraft to be fitted with a machine-gun, it was one of the earliest attempts to make an aircraft with offensive capability. A pusher-engined two-seater, the sesquiplane wings spanned 42 feet 6 inches (top) and 23 feet (bottom), and the length was 33 feet 9 inches. Designed by Horatio Barber with the aid of John D North, it was powered by a 90 hp Austro-Daimler six-cylinder engine with a 10-foot diameter chain-driven Chauvière propeller. The Colt Automatic gun was operated by the observer. It did not see any combat service.

Claude Grahame-White produced a strange single-seat biplane for racing and aerobatic work. Using the fuselage of a Morane-Saulnier monoplane and the wings from John North's Popular biplane – the Grahame-White Type VII, this was known only by the nickname 'Lizzie' or, sometimes, 'Tea Tray'. With a top wing-span of 28 feet 6 inches and lower of 14 feet, this single-bay machine first flew on November 22nd, 1913. Sometime in 1914, it was converted to a two-bay biplane with a greater-span lower wing. Here it is seen on its maiden flight in its first configuration. The engine was a 50 hp Gnôme air-cooled seven-cylinder driving a 7-foot 6-inch diameter propeller.

The 'Charabanc' biplane was Grahame-White's Type X. Designed by John Dudley North (1893-1968) for the sole purpose of carrying passengers, this accommodated four people in wicker seats behind the pilot. It was said at one time to have carried no fewer than eleven passengers. A two-and-a-half-bay sesquiplane, the top wing-spanned 62 feet and the engine was initially a 120 hp Austro-Daimler six-cylinder in-line water-cooled unit but this was later replaced by a 100 hp Green with a 9-foot 6-inch diameter Lang propeller. It was from this aircraft that the first parachute descent was made from a heavier-than-air machine in Britain on May 9th, 1914. Only one was ever built.

Early aircraft were destined to have but short lives and this tiny snapshot, salvaged from a pile of old photographs, shows Maurice Farman S.7 number 69, one of the machines used by the Naval Air Station, Great Yarmouth. It was flown from Hendon to its Norfolk base on May 31st, 1913 but in March 1914 it force-landed in this pasture where it instantly drew a curious crown of onlookers. Damaged in its unplanned descent, it was sent back to Hendon by road to be rebuilt. Delivered to Eastchurch in April, 1915, it crashed there on May 17th and was deleted.

With its 130 hp Clerget engine, Sopwith F.1 Camel N6339 was built at Kingston-upon-Thames and delivered from Brooklands to Dover for storage on May 18th, 1917. Damaged during delivery by lorry, it was rebuilt and delivered to the Royal Naval Air Service flying school at Cranwell by May 16th, 1918. Piloted by Capt Maxwell Hutcheon Findlay (1898-1936), it landed on top of another Camel during a training flight. People often wonder how this type of accident – surprisingly an all-too common incident – can happen. The answer is that it is the easiest of all training mishaps. Many aircraft flying the circuit and seeking to land in sequence, but if one machine makes a slightly higher than normal approach, he cannot see what is immediately beneath him. And if a lower machine is also concentrating on a landing approach, then the result is too often inevitable. There are dozens of recorded similar incidents, not all in training, either. Findlay went on to lose his life in the 1936 Johannesburg Air Race.

War is always a defining event in history. In recent times, it has also been a defining event in progress and nowhere was this clearer than during the First World War of 1914-1918. We entered the years of conflict barely able to fly, yet ended it with huge, heavy-duty, more-or-less reliable aircraft that could do things not dreamed off when peaceful times transformed into years of conflict and bloodshed. One can truthfully say that one of the beneficiaries of these hostilities was aviation. Handley Page responded to this era of force majeur with the biggest aircraft the world had yet seen. In fact, the words 'Handley Page' entered the dictionary between the wars with the definition of 'a very large aeroplane'. Here is a twin-engined O/400 bomber designed and built at Frederick Handley Pahe's Cricklewood factory in North London. Some 554 were built and here the prototype is being prepared for flight in 1915. The expertise gained in making these made the transition to passenger-carrying air-liners relatively simple.

Starting aircraft during the First World War relied on manual prop-swinging but as engines got bigger and more powerful, this task became more and more arduous. Also there were an increasing number of accidents. One man who solved the problem was Captain Bentfield Charles Hucks who devised the Hucks Starter, a conversion of a car to provide an adjustable-height shaft which could connect with a dog on the end of the aircraft engine crankshaft. As the car driver put the drive shaft into gear and accelerated his engine, so the shaft turned the engine effortlessly until it started. Introduced into RAF service just after the First World War, it enabled two men to start an engine from cold in 30

seconds and was far safer than the earlier method of swinging the propeller by hand. Hucks himself did not live to experience the acclaim that his invention earned for he was a victim of the dreadful influenza epidemic that raged across Europe in 1918-1919. This picture shows a replica being used to start a reconstructed SE.5A at Farnborough on August 24th, 1959.

Immediately after the First World War ended, aircraft manufacturers understandably envisaged a tremendous expansion of a civilian market based largely not so much on scheduled services as joy-riding. Westland, Grahame-White and Sopwith were ready with suitable designs which were quickly built. There was a problem, though. None had foreseen that with so many war-surplus aircraft available at dirt-cheap prices, the opportunities for expensive new aircraft was extremely limited. Indeed, the market was awash with practical aircraft which could, with varying degrees of ease, be converted into passenger-carriers. Here is one of the candidates for this outwardly attractive market – the sole example of the Sopwith Antelope. Powered by a 180 hp Hispano-Suiza Viper fitted with quickly detachable cowling, the Antelope had the luxury of a cockpit-operated engine self-starter by Black & Manson. The four-wheel undercarriage was to prevent the machine nosing over on landing. Based on an earlier machine – the Wallaby – it was built in 1919 and could carry two passengers in an enclosed cabin complete with door. Here it is pictured at roll-out. With a speed range from 38 to 100 mph, it was shown at Olympia in July 1920 where it created a good impression and then, later that year, it was given a revised landing gear (just two wheels) and tapered ailerons, In this state it was entered for the Air Ministry's Small Commercial Aeroplane Competition of 1920 staged at Martlesham Heath and gained second prize, the first going to Westland's Limousine. The engine was by then a 200 hp Wolseley Hispano Viper, said to give an 'actual output' of 210 hp at 2,100 rpm. Gaining a C of A on August 10th, 1920, it became G-EASS and, like the earlier Wallaby, was later sold to Australia becoming G-AUSS.

Here is a later view of the Antelope with its civil markings. G-EASS got its C of A on August 10th, 1920, and was shipped out to Sopwith's sister company, Larkin Aircraft Supply Co, in Melbourne, Australia in April 1923 where it became G-AUSS, later VH-USS. It enjoyed a long and productive life 'down-under' and flew until withdrawn from use as late as February 1935.

Despite its load-carrying capabilities, one of the least attractive passenger conversions of a First War aircraft was that of the Blackburn Kangaroo. Introduced in 1918, the aircraft was not without structural concerns and the rear fuselage tended to twist under tailplane loads. Even so, it was not fully retired until 11 years later. Of the 20 built, a number hit the civilian market, amongst them B9985 pictured here. It was operated by Grahame-White Aviation Co Ltd at Hendon becoming G-EADG in June 1919. It was scrapped on C of A expiry just two years later. The passenger in the extreme nose had a great view and was always the first to get hurt in a mishap.

It seems unthinkable today that one could take fare-paying passengers in an aircraft that was barely airworthy, yet that is just what used to happen. Here is a joy-ride ticket for a flying pageant staged at Edinburgh's Turnhouse Aerodrome on March 20th 1913. An extra 5/- would buy you a 'stunt flight' and the hope that the aircraft would hold together during the manoeuvre!

By the 1920s, companies like de Havilland at North London's Stag Lane aerodrome were operating more reliable machines. Air Taxis Ltd was a subsidiary company of de Havilland.

Besides heavier-than-air machines, there was still a significant following for the airship which would be sustained right up into the 1930s until first the R101 tragedy of October 1930 and, finally, the Hindenburg in May 1937. Airships were always in a different class being unwieldy, labour-intensive to operate and totally subservient to weather conditions. There were prenty of precedents for this. The R33, pictured here, first flew on March 6th, 1919, and went to RAF Pulham in Norfolk. Between then and mid-October, it made 23 flights totalling 337 flying hours. In 1920, it was civilianised becoming G-FAAG. All went well until April 16th 1925 when a storm blew up, the R33 broke its moorings and, with only a skeleton crew aboard, was blown out over the North Sea. The nose partially collapsed and deflated the first gas-cell as pictured here. The adventure was not over and R33 found herself over the Dutch coast from whence the slow chug home to Norfolk took until the next day.

Despite many reservations, the 'airship camp' remained strong as the 1920s closed. Two great airships were being built – the R100 by private contract and the Government-backed R101. On October 12th, 1929, the R101 was finished and, as pictured here, removed from her shed at Cardington to be moored at the specially-built 'giant' mast for the first trials which called for a 48-hour tether without problem before her maiden flight. Almost exactly a year later, R101 would crash and burn taking with her some of the top people in Britain's aviation industry.

The very first civil aircraft registrations comprised a three-digit number preceded by the letter K. One hundred and sixty-nine aircraft were thus marked before the 'G' system emerged on which occasion all the 'K' aircraft (the ones that hadn't already crashed) were re-marked with a G-E grouping. This Airco DH.9B was the prototype of the DH.9 three-seater conversion for one pilot and two passengers. Registered on April 30th, 1919, to Air Transport & Travel Ltd, K-109 was formerly H9277 and would undertake the first charter flight to Paris on July 15th. In due course this aircraft became G-EACC, was converted to a DH.9J in July 1926 and remained flying with the Stag Lane-based DH Flying School until December 1933. In this picture the aircraft is being used for aerial photography early in 1919.

A product of the Kilburn-based Central Aircraft Company, the Centaur IV was the first original design to be built by the firm. Designed by Anthony Archibald Fletcher (1887-1950), there were three versions. The Centaur IV was a two-seat side-by-side dual-control open cockpit aircraft, the IVA a single-pilot version for two passengers, and the IVB with floatplane landing gear. Eight aircraft were built but, as there was at this time no market for private ownership, all eight were all built as three-seaters. The prototype had a 70 hp (52 kW) Renault air-cooled V-8 engine but the seven  production aircraft were fitted with Anzani. All were initially used by Central Aircraft for joyriding and instruction at Northolt Aerodrome. The fifth aircraft was fitted with a three-float undercarriage. It was used for a week giving joyrides at Southend-on-Sea before being converted into a landplane later in 1920. It crashed in October 1920. Several of the aircraft were sold in Belgium and some were still operating in 1938. The last to be built was G-EAQF, became O-BOTI, later OO-OTH, and was destroyed in the German invasion of Belgium in May, 1940.

After the Centaur IV, there were two variants of the Centaur IIA, one with an open cockpit as seen here, and one with a cabin enclosure. G-EAHR accommodated two pilots and six passengers. Again the designer was Fletcher. Like its predecessor it was built for joy-riding but was somewhat larger. Registered G-EAHR, it first flew during July 1919 piloted by Frank T Courtney. This machine was destroyed in July 1920 in a thoroughly avoidable accident when it attempted to take off from Northolt Aerodrome with crossed elevator cables. The engines were 160 hp Beardmores.

The cabin version of the Central Centaur IIA could accommodate seven passengers and was registered G-EAPC in May, 1920. Entered in the Air Ministry's Commercial Aircraft Competition of 1920, it was unplaced. The verdict on it was that it was under-powered and old-fashioned and when it was loaded up with the fuel required for the three-and-a-half hour test-flight it was unable to carry either passengers or pilot! This machine crashed on September 25th, 1920, at Sharvel Lane, Hayes, Middlesex, just 1,500 yards from its take-off from Northolt Aerodrome. The pilot lost control and the aircraft spun, killing all six on board including Central's 22-year-old chief pilot, Lt Frederick Benjamin Goodwin-Castleman and a 14-year-old girl. No further examples were made and Central Aircraft closed down in May, 1926.

One of Sopwith's earliest post-war products was the two-seat single-engined long-range Wallaby biplane. A 'two-and-a-half' bay machine, it was designed to compete in an Australian government-sponsored contest for an England to Australia flight which would earn its winner a £10,000 prize. Powered by a 360 hp Rolls-Royce Eagle VIII engine, it had the unusual feature of an open cockpit with two seats that could be retracted inside the enclosed cabin. The sole example, pictured here, was registered G-EAKS and left Hounslow for Australia on October 21st, 1919. Its participation in the contest was denied the two pilots by a chain of events that included bad weather, one arrest, damage in Persia and a crash-landing on the island of Bali in the Dutch East Indies on April 17th 1920. In the end it was shipped to Australia where it was rebuilt as an eight-seater transport for use by Australian Aerial Services Ltd as G-AUDU. Here is a rare view of it prior to its departure from Hounslow Heath.

The Austin Motor Company was an important manufacturer of aircraft during and after the First World War. The company made a handful of practical aircraft post-war, but none entered production because the market for new aircraft was swamped by the vast numbers of government surplus war production aircraft that flooded the market. Austin's last attempt to break into a civil market was with the side-by-side two-seat Kestrel, G-EATR. Designed by John Kenworthy as an entrant for the Air Ministry's 1920 competition, the Kestrel came third in the small aeroplane class winning its makers the useful sum of £1,500. It had a tubular steel fuselage and folding wings. Power was provided by a 160 hp Beardmore. Despite its attractiveness, orders were not forthcoming. Herbert Austin, head of the company, decided to close down the aircraft business and concentrate on the cars, so the sole Kestrel was offered for sale, with spares, in May, 1924. It was sold to Fraser's Flying School, Kingsbury, Wembley, London but was not flown. When Kingsbury Aerodrome closed in that same year to make room for building, the Kestrel was broken up.

The first London Airport was at a Cavalry ground on Hounslow Heath but this was replaced in 1920 by Croydon. This field opened as early as December 1915 as Beddington Aerodrome on one side of Plough Lane, and Waddon Aerodrome on the other. Waddon was opened in 1918 as part of the adjoining National Aircraft Factory No. 1, to facilitate test and delivery flights of newly-built aircraft. The airfield at Beddington became a training ground for the Royal Flying Corps and when the war ended it was retained, becoming a training airfield for the newly formed Royal Air Force. Now the two airfields were amalgamated and to become Croydon Aerodrome, the gateway for all international flights to and from London. Eventually Plough Lane would be closed and the two airfields made into one large area with the main terminal on the east side off Purley Way. This was opened on May 2nd, 1928. The original airport, inaugurated on March 29th, 1920, was rather a shanty town as seen in this contemporary view.

The Avro 504K was originally designed as a trainer aircraft and large numbers were used by the Royal Air Force. This one, G-EAWI, was originally E3672 and was awarded its first C of A on March 1st, 1921. Along with seven other similar aircraft (G-EAWI, G-EAWJ, G-EBOF, G-EBOY, G-EBRB, G-EBTF, and G-AAGB), it was owned and operated by Surrey Flying Services Ltd where it was used for training as well as providing joy-rides. On September 9th, 1921, it crashed on landing killing the pilot, the sole person on board.

Bernard Martin was a Nottingham-born aviator who served in the RFC and RAF during the First World War. Afterwards he bought a number of Airco DH.6 aircraft to start a touring joy-ride business. In 1920, he was awarded the joy-riding rights to Cleethorpes where this picture was taken on July 25th, 1923. Here he stands, left, with one of his aircraft, G-EAWT, and his crew. He also gained the concession for the Isle of Wight and operated there from fields that would much later become Bembridge Airport.

During this period, ex-Service aircraft were being given new roles in civil flying. However, not all aircraft were suitable. One tends to forget just how big some of these machines actually were. After the relatively compact DH.6 in the previous picture, here is one of the three Bristol Berkeley three-seat bomber aircraft powered by a 650 hp Rolls-Royce Condor engine. First flown in March 1925 and standing no less than 14 feet high, it was designed by Wilfrid Thomas Reid with the aid of Bristol's chief designer Frank Barnwell.

As aviation advanced, so, inevitably, there was an increasing number of accidents. Aside from the dreadful tragedies that notched up fatalities, some of these incidents were merely downright amusing. One such event happened at Croydon on the morning of August 27th, 1930, with a French night air-mail from Paris. Operated by Air Union, Farman F.61 Goliath *Normandie*, F-AECU, landed too far up the field and could not stop before hitting the corrugated iron fence that separated the airfield from Stafford Road. The huge biplane ended up on the tram-tracks and had to be pushed back onto the airfield by people-power. This news picture shows a large number of hands pushing the lower wing's leading edge. First registered on May 15th, 1922, *Normandie* saw service until its withdrawal from use in December, 1932.

While the name of Handley Page held the association with 'giant airliners', Vickers was not far behind. The Vimy heavy bomber was designed by Reginald Kirshaw 'Rex' Pierson, the company's chief designer. It was, however, right at the end of the war and by the time of the Armistice, none had actually seen war service. While the RAF was able to employ the Vimy profitably as a peacetime transport, the design paved the way for civilian use in the form of the Vimy Commercial. This had a larger-diameter fuselage and first flew from Joyce Green Airfield in Kent on April 13th, 1919. It carried the interim civil registration K-107 and was later re-registered as G-EAAV. The type went on to make history, though, when it began setting records for long-distance flights, in particular the first non-stop crossing of the Atlantic Ocean by John Alcock and Arthur Brown in June 1919. Other record-breaking flights were made from the United Kingdom to destinations such as South Africa and Australia. The Vimy continued to be operated until the 1930s in both military and civil capacities.

Just once in a while one finds a situation that is worth picturing even if the association with a core subject is but tenuous. This book has already shown a French airliner engaged with tram-tracks in Croydon, so let's have another non-British picture. This one is splendidly spectacular and shows a seaplane impaled on a typical 1900-style German roof-top. The aircraft is a seaplane made by Flugzeugbau Friedrichshafen GmbH, a company founded in 1912 by a former Zeppelin airship man, Theodor Kober. Although this firm only existed for around 14 years, it was a significant maker of seaplanes for the German Navy's Marine-Fliegerabteilung as well as medium-range land-plane bombers. Karl Gehlen was the chief of design. Wound up in 1923, it was absorbed by Dornier Flugzeugwerke. This picture dates from 1918.

The DH.51 was intended to be a low-cost three-seater dating from 1924 and powered by the 90 hp RAF 1A engine. Large numbers of these engines were available very cheaply as war surplus. However, this motor only came as a single-ignition model so the aircraft was ineligible for a C of A. De Havilland had little choice but to re-engine the aircraft with the far more expensive – but certifiable – dual ignition ADC Airdisco air-cooled V8. This gave the aircraft a considerably improved performance but it was no longer cheap to operate. As a result, only three aircraft were constructed. The first was a single-bay biplane designated the DH.51A. It was exported to Australia and later converted to a floatplane as the DH.51B. The other two aircraft were two-bay machines like G-EBIQ pictured here. The first owner was Air Commodore James George Weir (1887-1973), the famed Scottish aviator and airman who went on to finance Juan de la Cierva's development of the autogiro and to head up one of Scotland's major engineering companies still in existence today. The DH.51 survived until December 1933 when it was scrapped at Hanworth.

Hardly an attractive machine, the Vickers Vulcan was a single-engined passenger-carrier created in 1922 for Instone Air Line and Imperial Airways. Designer by 'Rex' Pierson and built at Brooklands, Surrey, the first flight took place in April 1922 at the hands of company chief test pilot, Stanley Cockerell. Based on the Vimy bomber but with a huge fuselage and only one engine (a Rolls-Royce Eagle VIII), nine machines were built. G-EBLB pictured here was the last to be delivered and went to Imperial Airways on May 12th, 1925. On July 13th, 1928, it took off from Croydon on a test-flight to check on a newly-fitted engine. Five members of staff went along for the joy-ride. Just after take-off the engine water temperature went above 100deg.C and power was lost. The aircraft crashed into a potato field near Leigh Cottage on Croydon's Woodcote Road. The pilot, Captain John Spafford, was able to escape and rescue one passenger before the aircraft burst into flames, killing the other four.

The history of this, the oldest surviving DH.60 Moth, would make a good novel on its own! Awarded its C of A on August 20th, 1925, G-EBLV was acquired by the Woodford-based Light Planes (Lancashire) Ltd and used for pilot training but by August of 1938 it was in private ownership living in a field. At some time it was allegedly flown by Alan Cobham but on February 5th, 1939, it crashed at Castle Bromwich and was declared to be damaged beyond repair. The wreckage was acquired by de Havilland at Hatfield and stored all through the war. In 1952 it was taken on as a project by students of the de Havilland Technical Collage at Hatfield who sympathetically rebuilt it. Subsequently it lived in the main hangar at Hatfield where it shared space with, at various times, the Comet, DH Heron, Trident and later BAC aircraft. Today this venerable old girl is preserved at Old Warden's Shuttleworth Collection.

This DH.60 Moth, G-EBOU, was fitted with a 50 hp Genet 1 radial in order to take part in the 1926 Lympne Lightplane trials. Flown by Hubert Stanford Broad, unfortunately an oil-leak meant that it was unplaced. It subsequently took part in various club races with varying success until in 1927 it was sold to a former First World War flying ace, Canadian-born Flying Officer Frank Ormond 'Mongoose' Soden (1895-1961) who was credited with 27 victories. Following a brief aerobatic career, it was sold to Germany as D-1651. Here Soden is seen piloting his single-seat Moth

While Avro had their Avian, and de Havilland the Moth, Westland had their Widgeons. Unlike the other two, this was a high-wing strut-braced monoplane and a variety of different types emerged from Yeovil in Somerset. This one, G-EBPW, was a Mk.III. It had a distressingly short life. Gaining its C of A on April 12, 1927, it was registered to Robert A Bruce of Westland. On June 6th, the aircraft was competing in a race at Bournemouth. The pilot, Laurence Pratt Openshaw, was Bruce's son-in-law. Without warning, the Widgeon collided with a Bluebird I, G-EBKD flown by Sqn Ldr Walter Longton. Both aircraft crashed at Ensbury Park Racecourse, Bournemouth, and burst into flames killing the pilots. Openshaw had only been married three weeks: his wife witnessed the accident as did that of Longton.

Engine guru Major Halford had played a vital part in the development and production of almost all the inline engines from the First World War onwards. Famously cutting engines in half to make smaller and practical lightplane motors, in 1928 he worked his magic in reverse by taking two Gipsy I engines and uniting them with a common crankcase. The upshot was an eight-cylinder V-engine which de Havilland of Stag Lane Aerodrome named the Ghost, It turned out 198 hp for a lighter weight than the old Renault V-engines that lay at the heart of the Gipsys. It was developed for the new four-seat cabin DH.75 Hawk Moth. But when Hubert S Broad flew the prototype, G-EBVV, pictured here, on December 7th, 1928, it was underpowered and the performance was not up to scratch. The answer was the 240 hp Armstrong Siddeley Lynx VIA – but even with this the Hawk Moth was down on performance.

Being down on power did not prevent the prototype Hawk Moth from posing for a good picture. This one, shot by the staff photographer of the weekly magazine *The Aeroplane*, was taken in December 1928. Initially, there had been plans to call the aircraft the DH Moth Six but the name never stuck and Hawk Moth was the popular choice.

As it was, the Hawk Moth would be tried with a variety of engines after the Ghost and the Lynx. The 300 hp Wright Whirlwind J-5 was tried in one sold to the Canadian market, another had a 350 hp Armstrong Siddeley Cheetah IX. This one, which remained unregistered, flew with a 300 hp Wright Whirlwind R-975 and was aimed at the American market. But the sales people at de Havilland were up against strong competition from established US makers, in particular from Ryan with its B-1 Brougham. As it was, just ten aircraft were laid down, only eight of which were ever finished.

Avro 594 Avian III G-EBWK got its C of A in March 1928 and spent most of its early life in the flying club world of Lancashire before coming south to the Bedford School of Flying at Barton-in-the-Clay in October 1938. After the expiry of its C of A on June 30th, 1939, the aircraft was declared 'written off' as 'disposed of in parts' by December 19th, 1940.

The Bristol 89A Trainer of 1926 was used by the Reserve School of Flying at Filton until C of A expiry in October 1933. A two-seat advanced trainer, it was a direct development from the Bristol Jupiter fighter with oleo undercarriage and enlarged horn-balanced rudder to allow for the torque of the 320 hp Bristol Jupiter IV engine. Just 23 were built and today none survive. The example here, G-EBYL, was used in 1930 to try out Handley Page's leading-edge slots seen fitted to the upper wings.

The first of the 'G-A' registrations went to this DH-60G Moth registered on September 12th 1928 to Captain Geoffrey de Havilland at Stag Lane Aerodrome, Edgware. Temporarily fitted with a closed or coupé cabin top, de Havilland and his wife took this machine on a 4,600-mile round trip to Morocco and back between the 3rd and the 29th of March, 1929. It was sold soon afterwards to Ivor H McClure as an open-cockpit aircraft as pictured here. Later it went to the Yorkshire Aeroplane Club and was based at Yeadon. When the 1939-45 war broke out, it was used as a dummy aerodrome decoy – a sad end for a once-great aeroplane.

Although only 26 were built, the Westland Widgeon was one of the bright stars of the late 1920s. Introduced in 1924, the Mk.I was aimed at the two-seat light plane contest at Lympne, first flying on September 22nd that year. With its 1,090cc Blackburne Thrush engine it was underpowered and later crashed. Rebuilt and converted into the Mk.II with a 60 hp Armstrong Siddeley Genet radial, the Widgeon suddenly began to show its mettle. The company decided to put the parasol monoplane into production aimed at the private owner. The outcome was the Widgeon Mk.III, the first of which made its maiden flight in March of 1927. The engine could be either a Genet or an inline Cirrus such as that seen here in G-AADE which was first registered on March 6th, 1929, to Carrill Stanley Napier. Its last public appearance was at the Skegness Aero Pageant in May 1932. And then, on September 7th, Napier was taking off from Yeovil bound for Shoreham, where he lived when disaster struck. An uncontrollable swing on take-off and the Widgeon cartwheeled into history. Here, in happier times, it seems to hang on its wing slots.

Pictured at Stag Lane Aerodrome in March, 1929, is newly-C of A'd DH.60G Gipsy Moth G-AAEA. Sold to Mrs Franklin Spencer Cleaver (1885-1935), a notable aviatrix who named it *Will o' the Wisp*. The daughter of Northern Ireland's first Minister of Finance, Hugh MacDowell Pollock, she married Lieutenant-Colonel Arthur Spencer Cleaver and, in 1929, spent three months flying this aircraft to India and back, returning to Croydon Airport on June 10th. Her pilot was Captain Donald Drew of Imperial Airways. By July 1933, she was responsible for a flying display which was held at Aldergrove Aerodrome, Co. Antrim with the intention of stimulating air-mindedness in Ulster. Her biographer described her as making 'the usually fatiguing journey to Northern Ireland three or four times a year in her own aeroplane, and, fitted with extra tanks to save refuelling during the day, it has many times enabled her to breakfast in London, shop in Paris from 11 to 1, and return in plenty of time for dinner at her house in London'. By March of 1933 the Moth was owned by Philips & Powis Aircraft (Reading) at Woodley and later it went to a new owner in Baldonnel, Co. Dublin, as EI-AAR where it crashed in December 1934 and was no more.

Cierva C.19 Mk.II G-AALA was built by A V Roe & Co Ltd at Hamble as an Avro Type 620. Powered by an Armstrong Siddeley Genet Major I of 105 hp, it gained its C of A on Christmas Eve, 1929. A feature of this aircraft was its ability to land at high angles of attack and it was quickly found that under these circumstances the initial touchdown was on the bottom corners of the rudders. The outcome was the C.19 Mk III which had rudders that were significantly more tapered to clear the ground on landing. At the same time, the rotor diameter was increased by five feet. Here the machine is pictured running up at Hanworth in 1931. The following May, this autogyro would be written off in a ground resonance incident.

This DH.60G Gipsy Moth G-AALK was built as a coupé as shown here and registered to The Rt Hon Frederick Edward 'Freddie' Guest (1875-1937) on September 10th, 1929. Guest was a notable politician and Chief Whip of Lloyd George's Coalition Liberal Party, 1917–1921. He was also Secretary of State for Air between 1921 and 1922. A keen amateur pilot, in 1930 he became Deputy Master of the Guild of Air Pilots and Air Navigators, and Master in 1932. The Moth was used on The Guest Expedition to Africa in January-February 1930 flown by Guest's pilot, Miss Winifred Spooner. The Moth's cabin-top was subsequently removed and its last owner was Brooklands pilot Arthur Edward Dobell. He had the misfortune to crash the much-travelled Moth at Shankend Station, Hawick, Roxburghshire, writing it off on April 3rd, 1937.

A clear-cut case of 'Oh! Dear!' The Rev Frederick A Simpson of Fen Ditton, Cambridge, was rare amongst his fellow clergymen as being both a flying enthusiast and a private owner. Indeed, he purchased this fine Gipsy Moth from its Stag Lane factory in March, 1929. The difficulty was finding time to fly and looking after it. In the autumn of 1931, he realised that it was more than he could undertake along with his responsibilities as a man of the cloth. He agreed to sell it to Francis W Armitage who actually had very little money. However, sale on 'deferred terms' was agreed. Armitage proudly had his picture taken with his new Moth, reproduced here. He then flew from Cambridge to Blandford Forum but as he came in to land something unthinkable happened – the control column came loose in his hand. The Moth crashed and was damaged beyond repair. Armitage escaped badly shaken.

One of the losses in the history of aircraft preservation concerns this unusual aircraft designed and built by Australian record-breaking pilot Herbert J 'Bert' Hinkler at his home at Sholing, Southampton. The Ibis was an all-wood cantilever shoulder-wing monoplane powered by two Salmson radials arranged in tandem, one as a tractor, the second as a pusher. A close co-operation with AV Roe of Hamble and, in particular, designer Rowland Henry Bound, led to its creation which, while built as a landplane, was ultimately intended to be an amphibian. The wing was the work of Basil B Henderson of Hendy Aircraft. First flown during May 1930, it was subsequently dismantled and stored at Hinkler's house at Thornhill Park. Hinkler's death in his Puss Moth in January 1933 sealed the fate of the machine which, while registered G-AAIS, never carried these markings. Discovered semi-derelict and less its engines in Hinkler's garden in September 1952, it was acquired by one H C G Stisted who renovated the airframe and exhibited it at the Hatfield Garden Party on June 14th, 1953. Unable to secure storage space for this rare relic, it was broken up and burned at Lee-on-Solent in 1959.

Cirrus-engined DH.60X G-AAPA was the first of ten similar aircraft ('PA to 'PJ) block-booked by makers de Havilland to National Flying Services Ltd of Hanworth Aerodrome, Middlesex. The C of A was issued on August 17th, 1929 and the aircraft was operated by Hull Aero Club, Hedon, which was part of National Flying Services Ltd. After National Flying Services failed, due to bankruptcy, G-APAA was re-registered on June 27th, 1933, to William F Forbes-Sempill, The Master of Sempill, Hanworth Aerodrome, but was still operated by the Hull Club. In March 1935, full ownership was transferred to the Hull club by sale. All went well until July 17th, 1935; the aircraft was performing a loop when it went out of control, entered a spin and crashed at Westlands near Hedon. Pilot Albert Bishop Croskin was injured but his 26-year-old passenger, Keith Leonard Atkin, was killed. The Moth was damaged beyond repair.

Imperial Airways operated a large number of flying boats, in particular on sections of its long-distance routes. G-AASJ was a Short S.8/1 Calcutta named *City of Khartoum*. Used on the Genoa to Palestine and Alexandria sections of the India and South Africa routes, it gained its C of A on January 13th 1930 and survived until the last day of 1935 when the pilot's worst nightmare came true – it ran out of fuel in darkness and crashed within sight of the flarepath at Alexandria inbound from Athens. The aircraft split its hull on striking the water and sank, drowning nine passengers and three of the crew. The only survivor was Captain Vernon Gorry Wilson. This pilot survived a second night-time descent through fuel-shortage with Qantas, Imperial's Australian partner. The picture shows a pristine 18-seat G-AASJ moored off the manufacturer's slipway prior to a flight to Cairo to re-establish the lapsed portion of the Mediterranean passenger section of the London-India Air Mail route.

This Avro 619 Five, G-AASO, was built at the company's Newton Heath, Manchester, works and first registered on November 14th, 1929. It was the first of two Avro Fives to see service in the UK and was the Avro demonstrator. It was entered for the 1930 King's Cup Race on July 5th, 1930, by Sir Philip Sassoon. Flown in the event by Flight Lieutenant Sydney Leo Gregory Pope, it proved not to be a born racer and quietly retired at Woodford. That September it was re-registered to Wilson Airways Ltd of Nairobi, Kenya, as a replacement for its second machine, VP-KAE *Knight of the Grail*. While it was allotted the marks VP-KAH, these were never used and it flew as G-AASO on the African services until January 18th, 1932, when it was damaged beyond repair in a forced landing some 12 miles from its destination while en route from Salisbury to Broken Hill.

The three-seat Desoutter Mk.I G-AATF was registered in January 1930 and was one of the early models based on the Dutch Koolhoven FK-21 and built by the Desoutter Company at Croydon. Initially it served with Air Taxis Ltd but when the type was ill-advisedly put forward for the National Flying Services at Hanworth it was transferred there. And when NFS folded, it was re-registered to Laurence Aldred Mervyn Dundas, Earl of Ronaldshay, Portsmouth, The aircraft stayed at Hanworth. On May 9th, 1934, and with a full load of three large fellows on board, the 105 hp Cirrus Hermes-powered wooden aircraft attempted take-off. Instead of positioning the aircraft for maximum run, John Daniel Kerwin started his take-off run from the middle of the airfield…

G-AATF left the ground in a stalled state just short of the perimeter, struck a garden fence, ploughed through a back garden and stood on its nose against the side of a house in a tangle of gathered-up fence palings. Miraculously it didn't catch fire, the house was not damaged and nobody was killed. Pilot Kerwin was unhurt but his two passengers, aviation author William Courtenay and a Dutch friend, F Hoofa, were injured. The Desoutter was beyond repair.

The HP.42 is probably the world's most famous airliner. It is remembered as having been ordered 'straight off the drawing-board', a practice that became increasingly common in the 1930s as Imperial Airways strove to find the biggest and best passenger, freight and mail-carrying aircraft. Which makes it even more of a curio since only eight were built – four for what was called the Eastern routes, and four Western. There's an interesting tale about these 18 – 24 seaters. Frederick Handley Page was not keen on bracing wires which he considered fiddly and offering increased opportunity for rigging problems. No, he proclaimed. His HP.42 would have no bracing wires, only easily-fitted pin-jointed struts. Early on in the tests the diagonal bracing strut in the port outer bay buckled under an unsuspected twist that imposed a large compression load. Old man 'HP' quietly dropped his terse epithet on wires and from then on all '42' outer bays had diagonal wires… Here we see G-AAUD, a '42E' on the airfield at Nairobi. Named *Hanno*, this entered service with Imperial Airways on July 30th, 1931 and survived until wrecked by a gale at Bristol's Whitchurch Airport on March 19th, 1940.

F G Miles began his aviation career with his company Southern Aircraft Ltd at Shoreham. Here he took the concept of the Avro Baby and reworked it into a series of small biplanes which he called the Martlet of which eight were built, each slightly different. This one, G-AAYZ with its distinctive stub exhausts on its Gipsy II upright engine, first saw the light of day in June 1930 but was scrapped in 1937. Wing-span was just 25 feet and maximum speed 130 mph.

The Croydon-built Robinson Redwing was a delightful side-by-side two-seater of the 1930s. The prototype, G-AAUO seen here at roll-out in May 1930, was powered by a 75 hp ABC Hornet flat-four. Promoted as costing only £575 – cheaper than a Stag Lane Moth – with its wings folded, it was capable of being housed in a ten-feet wide garage while possessing a cruising speed of almost 100 miles an hour. Production models had the 80 hp Genet IIA five-cylinder radial as a lighter and more reliable power unit. Redwing had one weak spot – the joint where the undercarriage compression strut united with the fuselage top longeron, the wing centre-section pylon and the top bearer of the engine mount. In several well-documented instances, a heavy landing could result in major if not terminal airframe damage. This one suffered just that at Shoreham on March 11th, 1933. Although written off, its component parts kept several other Redwings flying just that little bit longer.

The DH.75 Hawk Moth underwent some subtle changes since the Ghost-powered prototype G-EBVV flew early in December, 1928. The original parallel-chord wings were increased in span from 44 to 47 feet, the span step-tapered increasing the area from 277 sq.ft to 334 sq.ft. With the installation of the Armstrong Siddeley Lynx VIA radial of 140 hp, the new variant was designated the DH.75A. G-AAUZ was the last DH.75A built. First flown in June 1932, it was initially operated by DH's sister company, Air Taxis Ltd, until sold abroad in December 1938.

Here is a curious snapshot. Two DH 60 Gipsy Moths, G-AAVJ and G-ABEV, yet both these registrations were allocated to Blackburn Bluebird Mk.IV aircraft. Neither was taken up and so both were re-allocated. 'AVJ was later exported becoming NC537N while 'BEV went on to become N4203E and then, later, HB-OKI then CH-217.

DH.60 G Gipsy Moth G-AAWO dates from May, 1930, and had a long and colourful life. Initially used by Scottish airlines pioneer Captain Edward E Fresson for survey flights around the Scottish islands, stored at Inverness during the war years and flew again in peacetime. Between 1949 and its rebuild in 1953 the fuselage was 'replaced' with that of G-AAHI, the original markings 'AWO being retained. The aircraft still flies, one of the few wooden Moths still gracing our skies.

The DH.80A Puss Moth was a popular touring mount and G-AAXT, which first flew in June, 1930, was the property of The Hon Brian Lewis at Aldenham Aerodrome, Hertfordshire. This would much later be better known as Elstree Aerodrome. In January, 1937, it was sold to France where it became F-APZX. Here it is pictured at Brooklands in July, 1930 shortly after it gained its first C of A. Although the early Puss Moths had a dubious safety record, there are still a number of these flying today.

The annual Royal Air Force Pageant at Hendon was a high-spot of the inter-war years. From July 8th, 1932, comes this view of some of the crowds watching a fly-past by a Westland-Hill Pterodactyl and one of the then-latest twin-tailed Cierva C.19 Autogiros. The picture is taken looking east towards the railway embankment and just visible distant right is the curved roof of one of the three big hangars. The hangar in view plus its adjacent second one is now the home of the RAF Museum. The third, most southerly one, was burned down in the early 1930s.

Something happened between 1934 and 1936 which was to have a profound effect on light aircraft. It was such a change that many owners of older aircraft had them updated. It concerned wheels and tyres. The early aircraft were fitted with very narrow wheels rather like those on this DH Puss Moth, G-AAZO. A legacy from the earliest times, many were still in the form of spoked wheels with canvas or aluminium hub dishes. The reasoning was that they had a low air-resistance (drag) but the downside was that they gave a rather rough ride over grass. Palmer Cord wheel and tyres dominated the 1920s and early 1930s. Then came the invention first of the Goodyear Aerowheel and then Dunlop's British-made aerowheel which included a brake drum integral with the cast aluminium hub. These tyres were fatter but gave a noticeably smoother ride on rough terrain. Aspiring aircraft purchasers were assured they were 'safer'… By the way, G-AAZO was impressed as AX870 but was written off on June 18th, 1941 while landing at Swindon when it struck a tar-sprayer.

G-ABAG is another DH.60G Gipsy Moth with a long and fascinating history. Built at Stag Lane in June, 1930, it was first owned by Bentley Motors Ltd and based at Heston. Here it was flown by a number of people including Amy Johnson. It competed in the 1931 King's Cup Race before being sold to a film company which used it to make early aerial movies of London and the Home Counties.

Then it was sold to a novice flyer, a leading optometrist named John Myles Bickerton (1894-1977) who bought the aircraft for £450 and made his first solo in it at Hanworth. He now sought out a piece of private land for his new-found aircraft and hobby. So was established Hawksridge Aerodrome, a plateau of well-drained high ground above Denham in Buckinghamshire. This eventually became today's Denham Aerodrome. In this picture by George Cull, the Moth is arranged as a single-seat for a post-war race.

Bickerton flew his beloved G-ABAG for several years before, in September 1934, selling it to one of his Hanworth instructors for £325. It had several more owners before the war and eventually it was acquired by the Shuttleworth Trust where, restored to perfection as a two-seater, it still flies today.

Powered by the 115 hp Cirrus Hermes II in-line upright engine, the Spartan two- and three-seaters were the production version of the original Simmonds Spartan designed with interchangeable wings and control surfaces. This feature was dropped for this later variant. G-ABAZ was the first of 19 examples built at Cowes on the Isle of Wight between 1930 and 1932. Named *Island Queen*, it was owned and operated by Sandown & Shanklin Flying Services Ltd and used for joy-riding. The red and silver three-seater was based at Shanklin's, now-lost, Apse Heath Aerodrome off Manor Road. Head of the enterprise was local garage owner Harry C Coombs. On the outbreak of war it was widely rumoured that the aircraft had been converted into a glider but exhaustive investigation has not elucidated any evidence.

DH.80 Puss Moth G-ABDF first saw the light of day in July 1930. In 1933 it took part in the King's Cup Race but was eliminated in Round 2. The pilot on this occasion was Arthur Patrick Kilvington Hattersley who would lose his life in the night-time crash of Fokker F.12 G-AEOT at Tilgate Forest, four miles south of Gatwick. G-ABDF survived the war in storage and was restored by Group Captain John Travers Mynors of RAF Sealand. In February 1954 it was taken over by DH apprentices at Hatfield who named themselves The Ellenbrook Club. They had it rebuilt as a two-seater, permanently removing the third seat. The work was undertaken at Elstree by Simpsons Aerospares Ltd and, painted crimson and black, the Moth became a notable visitor at local airfields. On May 29th, 1955, while on short final to RAF Great Dunmow, the aircraft stalled and crashed at Easton Lodge, about 400 metres from the airfield. The aircraft was destroyed by fire. Despite being a two-seater, there were three on board, all of whom were killed.

Avro 616 Sports Avian G-ABEE got its maiden C of A on December 12th, 1930, and survived the war to fly regularly with The Vintage Group at Denham. It was one of four Avians still existing, the others being G-EBZM, G-ACGT and G-ACKE, of which 'BEE and 'CKE were the least airworthy. The latter was damaged beyond economic repair on July 27th, 1950, at Coventry's Baginton Airport when it was involved in a ground collision with Tiger Moth G-AHKZ. In this picture from the 1950s, G-ABEE is arranged as a single-seater for a race, but for the majority of its post-war years it was a two-seater. Ultimately it was taken to White Waltham to await a C of A overhaul. While parked in an open blister hangar, 'aircraft spotters' removed fabric, instruments and fittings from the aircraft. Now shortage of repair funds saw the aircraft sold to Australia where bits were used to keep G-EBZM still flying. Overall a sad story.

First flown on February 29th, 1929, the Westland IV and later Wessex was a light passenger transport. The first model, G-EBXK, carried a crew of two and four passengers and was powered by 95 hp ADC Cirrus engines. The second model had three 105 hp Cirrus Hermes I engines and a metal rear fuselage. The two original Westland IVs were subsequently converted to Wessex standard powered by three 105 hp Armstrong Siddeley Genet Major radials. One example had 140 hp Genet Major 1A engines. While any attempt at streamlining was clearly far from the designer's brief, the Wessex was a sound and practical machine. Ten aircraft in total were built of which G-ABEG was the fifth in October 1930. Operated by Imperial Airways, it was damaged beyond repair at Chirindu, Rhodesia, in 1936.

G-ABEG was known in Westlands as the 'high-performance Wessex' and this 1931 photograph gives a good close-up of one of its 7-cylinder Genet Major engines as well as undercarriage detail. The Wessex was noted for its reliability and ability to operate with short take-off and landing runs – later to be called STOL. This made it attractive to Sir Alan Cobham in 1935 when he was looking for a small airliner to use for a service between Guernsey and the British mainland. Previously, flying boats had provided a service between Portsmouth and St Peter Port on the island. There was no public airfield at the time on Guernsey, only the private airfield at L'Erée run by the Guernsey Aero Club, of which Cobham was a member. The Wessex was certified as the only commercial aircraft to use L'Erée. Cobham's airline, Cobham Air Routes Ltd, used no fewer than four of these aircraft.

Avro 616 Sports Avian G-ABIB was issued with its first C of A on January 24th, 1931. It was used as a communications machine by British Petroleum Company Ltd of Finsbury Circus, London. The engine was a 115 hp ADC Cirrus Hermes II. This aircraft was sold to India in November 1933 as VT-AEV. In its day the Avian was almost as popular as de Havilland's Moth and Avro went on to build 405 examples.

Australian-born Arthur Leighton Angus, lived in Chippenham, Wiltshire. Blessed with inherited wealth, he had ideas for a novel type of aeroplane. Of very idiosyncratic structure, his ideas made use of mixed wood and metal construction. The upshot was an open single-seater powered by a 40 hp Salmson AD.9 radial. He registered it G-ABIK on January 23rd, 1931, and named it *Angostura*. Built at Hamble, he took it to Hanworth Aerodrome where he test flew it in early 1931. After the first flight at the beginning of March he made three or four further flights. At 3.15 pm on Saturday, March 21st, he took off and climbed to a height of about 100-150 feet whereupon he entered a steep left turn which became an almost vertical roll, at the end of which the Aquila fell with a sheer dive towards the ground. Angus, 26 years old, was killed. Writing of the mishap in *The Aeroplane*, C G Grey was moved to pen 'Mr Angus was a most amiable young man, and there are so few young men of his type who want to build experimental machines and have the money to do so…'

The 1930s were the hey-days of seaplanes, amphibians and flying boats and Cowes-based Saunders-Roe was one of the leading protagonists, two of the others being Blackburn and Short Brothers. Saunders-Roe, commonly abbreviated to Saro, made a significant number of different models that started with a small A.17 Cutty Sark, the A.19 Cloud and this, the A.21 Windhover. Only two examples of this attractive metal-hulled amphibian were built. Powered by three 120 hp Gipsy II upright engines, G-ABJP was used by The Hon Mrs Victor Bruce for her flight-refuelled endurance test in August, 1932. Named *City of Portsmouth* and with its distinctive little winglet fitted above the engines, this Windhover flew with Jersey Airways Ltd from 1935 until its withdrawal from service in 1938. *Picture by courtesy of British Hovercraft Corporation, Cowes.*

Wing-folding was one of the oldest features incorporated in biplanes as far back as the First World War. Originally offered as a feature of convenience and promoted widely as a design aspect in the Lympne Light Plane Trials, it was Geoffrey de Havilland who refined the system and offered it not so much as an attractive extra feature as a part of a basic aircraft specification. While wing-folding on a biplane or even a strut-braced high-wing monoplane was relatively simple and could be effected at little additional cost or weight penalty, folding wings on a cantilever monoplane was a whole different ballgame. DH succeeded, though, with the Moth Minor. In fact, from BA Swallow to Percival Proctor, the folding mechanism was seen as a standard part of an aircraft's specification. Today it is a rarity on factory-built aircraft. The picture shows Gipsy Moth G-ABJJ first flown in March 1932, a survivor of impressment (BK582), sold to Canada as CF-AAA, and now back dancing with the clouds in familiar territory.

In the years before people took an interest in preserving old aircraft, an aeroplane that was outwardly derelict invariably met its Valhalla pretty quickly. Such was the case with this DH.80A Puss Moth G-ABKZ which first flew in February 1932. Used initially by DH's own air taxi firm, it was eventually impressed as DR607. Restored for civil use in February 1946, it was neglected and found at Southend in May 1949. Unloved, unwanted – and a candidate for the eager flame of a match.

A long-forgotten aircraft of the 1930s was the Saro-Percival Mailplane triple-engined slim-cabined aircraft said to have been designed by Edgar Percival and built by Saunders-Roe on the Isle of Wight. It is my personal opinion that this was an important and overlooked milestone in commercial aviation for it generated the Spartan series of airliners. Percival's involvement was somewhat tenuous and he did not endear himself to the people at Cowes (see *Percival Aircraft: Edgar Percival, the Man & his Legacy*, Stenlake, 2013). Here we see the Mailplane being readied at Somerton for its first flight in March, 1931.

It may appear as heresy to assert that Edgar Percival was not a particularly good aircraft designer, but there remains no doubt that while Percival insisted that all designs were his, without the major contributions of men such as Basil Henderson (Hendy aircraft), Rowland Bound and Arthur Bage, the name of Percival would not be in the van of aircraft designers. And the Mailplane was a good example of Percival's adherence to the design principle of 'try and see'. With its three 120 hp Gipsy inverted engines and single small tail, the Mailplane was unable to fly a straight line. Percival's solution was to make a twin tail strut-braced to the long, slender fuselage. *Picture courtesy Saunders-Roe Archives*

Registered G-ABLI on April 17th, 1931, the Mailplane, bearing the Saro type classification of A.24, was set for a proving flight to India. The cabin access door was similar to that Percival used on his contemporary light aircraft. Excessive vibration was experienced in the cabin area with the result that a heavy bracing wire (20cwt flexible) was introduced from the junction of the fuselage top longeron and the upper engine-bearing of the main engine back to the upper inboard engine mounting attachments on the wing engines on each side. This cable would later be replaced by rigid, heavy-duty steel struts,

This picture is particularly interesting in that it shows the comparative area of the twin fins and rudders as originally fitted.

Pictured at Heston with the distinctive gas-holder visible above the starboard fin and rudder, the Mailplane is preparing for its flight to India and back. On the original print, the added bracing wire can be seen running from the nose engine to the wing-mounted starboard engine. The pilot reported the rudders to be heavy and tiring to use. There were two small and rather cramped passenger seats behind the pilot. Headroom was at a premium. Edgar Percival says he sold the design rights to Saunders-Roe and resigned from the project. In truth, his financial contribution to the alleged 'joint' project did not materialise and he parted from the company amidst phrases that no doubt included mention of things about 'darkening our doors' and entreaties not to be seen again.

In a final endeavour to ease the pilot's load the aerodynamic balances on both rudders were increased in area producing what looked like horns to the tail. While this helped a little it was still an aircraft that required too much leg-force to fly for a long period.

A rare in-flight shot of the Saro A.24 Mailplane in its final form as flown to India and back by pilot Thomas Neville Stack. The bracing wires between the nose and the wing-mounted engines has now been replaced with steel struts on each side of the front fuselage.

Pictured at Heston Airport in October 1932 on its return from India, the Mailplane was now known as the Spartan A.24 Mailplane, The added bracing struts either side of the nose have been replaced by larger cross-section streamlined steel tubes.

With the Mailplane scrapped in early 1933, Saunders-Roe used the experience gained to convert the Mailplane design into a practical airliner. The upshot was the Spartan Cruiser Mk.I. It retained the basic geometry of the earlier machine but had a larger fuselage to combat vibration, a single tail with large aerodynamic balance, and a spatted, low-drag undercarriage. In May 1932, the prototype, G-ABTY, was test-flown by Lt Col Louis Arbon Strange who found it much easier to fly than the A.24, without the excessive cabin vibration and with a responsive, lighter-to-use single rudder.

From the somewhat ungainly Mailplane, the six-seater was a far more business-like venture. With the cantilever wooden wing of the Cutty Sark and an all-metal fuselage, the prototype Cruiser was premiered at the very first SBAC Show staged at Hendon on June 27th, 1932.

On August 30th, The Cruiser was flown at the Spartan demonstration alongside the Mailplane for comparison. Later, test pilot L A Strange flew HRH the Prince of Wales (the future King Edward VIII) from Sunningdale to Croydon on September 22nd. Here we see the engines being started. The two mechanics are holding the starting handle which plugged into the bottom of the engine cowling for the procedure.

The Cruiser was sold to The Hon Mrs Victor Bruce and used by her company Commercial Air Hire to deliver newspapers between Croydon and Le Bourget. On May 11th, 1935, G-ABTY was returning empty to Croydon after taking an early morning load of papers to Paris, when engine trouble forced it to ditch in the sea off the Kent coast some eight miles north-west of Le Treport. The pilot, Flt Lt John Bernard Walter Pugh, of Haslemere, Surrey, and R F Burgess, of Hove, Sussex, wireless operator, were quickly rescued by the fishing-boat *Ave Maria*, from Port en Bessin. The boat did not have radio and it was an anxious day before their safety could be confirmed. The Spartan sank five minutes after their rescue. Only one Cruiser Mk.I aircraft was made. An improved version, Cruiser Mk.II, was built and production extended to 12 examples. Finally, there were three Cruiser Mk.III aircraft, this with sleek cabin glazing and trousered undercarriage. After production ceased in May, 1935, these continued in service until operators Spartan Air Lines was absorbed into British Airways.

Spartan Three-Seater G-ABLJ was first flown in July 1931 and saw service with Portsmouth, Southsea & IOW Aviation Ltd before joining the fleet of aircraft used by Yapton Aero Club, Ford, in September 1938. Later that year the Yapton club moved to Portsmouth. On the outbreak of war, the Spartan went to Tangmere as the personal mount of Fl Off A C Douglas at RAF Tangmere. In 1944 it was given to the local Air Training Corps – the 'kiss of death' for any aeroplane but seen by many as a necessary step to foster the continued progress of service aviation.

The Spartan Arrow was built at Cowes by Spartan Aircraft Ltd. The prototype G-AAWY was powered by a Hermes II upright engine and first flew in May 1930. This example, G-ABMK, was built as a floatplane for the Hon Arthur Ernest Guinness (1876-1949) and is pictured in its Cowes workshop prior to its completion and first flight on June 26th, 1931. It was sold to Norway as LN-BAS in July 1935

De Havilland DH.80A Puss Moth had a curious conception. The prototype was DH.80 G-AAHZ, a tandem two-seater with a flat-sided plywood-covered all-wood fuselage and two doors on the starboard side. Each seat was in its own compartment. The aircraft was powered by a Gipsy II modified to run 'upside down' – the first Gipsy inline inverted styled the Mk.III. The aircraft attracted immediate interest and the decision was taken to go into full production at Stag Lane. The production machine, however, would have a welded tubular steel fuselage, two tandem seats in one compartment and staggered slightly so that an occasional third seat could be fitted, and one door would be fitted on the port side. G-ABLS dated from May, 1931, and served with Aberdeen Flying School. It participated in the 1934 King's Cup Race when, flown by Owen Cathcart Jones, it finished ninth. From 1939 until 1968 it was stored at Dyce after which it was restored and still flies today in black and gold livery.

Avro 616 Avian IVM G-ABMO was created in August 1931 and served with Merseyside Aero & Sports Ltd and on the outbreak of war was impressed as 2070M. It is pictured here all pristine at its roll-out. The engine is the 105 hp Hermes I upright.

Robinson Redwing G-ABNX got its first C of A on March 12th, 1932 and was sold to Claude P Hunter who kept at Hooton. He was managing director of James Hunter of Chester. Hunter's business was levelling and seeding new aerodromes through a process they called 'Hunterising'. Airfields that the firm advertised as made by them extended from Shanklin's Apse Heath to Heston, the Great Western Aerodrome, private airfield of Sir Charles Fairey later to be known as Heathrow, and Gandar Dower's Dyce. Hunter's surfaces were famously smooth and Claude Hunter used the Redwing for testing his work. By 1939, the Redwing was owned by the College of Aeronautical Engineering at Redhill. During the war it was stored at Farnham before being found derelict by the author in a hangar full of redundant office furniture at Elstree. Just before the hangar was cleared and its contents burned by contractors, the author accidentally stole the unloved Redwing... G-ABNX went to safe storage at Panshanger in 1949 from whence it passed into the care of John Pothecary and E H Gould in December 1959 who painstakingly restored it and flew it extensively for the rest of the century. Based on his private airstrip at Slinfold, Surrey, it still flies to this day. The engine is the 80 hp Armstrong Siddeley Genet IIA radial.

Popularly known as 'The Big Moth', the DH.51 was a three-seater dating from 1925 powered by a 120 hp Airdisco, Three were built the last of which was G-EBIR *Miss Kenya* so named because in January 1926 it was taken to Nairobi. In September 1928 it took the odd markings G-KAA but the following January it became VP-KAA. In July 1965 the old aeroplane was found in Africa and in a major operation was dismantled, stowed aboard an RAF Blackburn Beverley and brought back to Britain as G-EBIR for the Shuttleworth Trust at Old Warden where this veteran of the world's skies still flies.

A French airliner with ten passengers landed at Croydon on June 18th, 1937. Finding himself rather a long way down the field and still rolling fast, the pilot 'stood on the brakes' but nothing happened. In front of him was a hangar and a Moth belonging to Surrey Flying Services. In desperation, the fellow in the cockpit kicked the rudder bar full over and opened up the engine on the opposite side in an attempt to skid the aircraft away from the obstruction. It didn't work and the fast-travelling aircraft swept up the innocent Moth pushing it sideway across the hangar apron until its starboard wings contacted the hangar doors which were closed. The poor Moth was neatly folded up and turned on its side in a heap. This picture was taken shortly after the French machine, now with damaged wing and a broken propeller, was pushed out of the way. First flown in August 1931, G-ABPC was rebuilt and flew again to be impressed as AX784 and, in December 1940, used by Sound City Films as a dummy airfield decoy. This DH.60G had been in trouble before: on July 10th, 1934, pilot Suhrid Mallik was practising forced landings at a field at Charlwood near Gatwick when he hit and killed 70-year-old farm worker Harry Knight.

American aircraft were unusual in the inter-war British skies. They were expensive imports despatched by sea and were unpopular with engineers because the usual British AGS parts (nuts, bolts, turnbuckles – you name it) did not fit. Mechanics all said 'They've got funny screw-threads!' and all spares had to come not from your average flying-club workshop but expensively from America. Which is why these aircraft were few and far between, like this 1931 four-seat Stinson Junior made at Wayne, Nebraska, in 1931. G-ABSU, originally 10897, was imported by Lt Col Edward Pardee Johnson in November that year and kept at Heston. He in turn passed it on to Lt Col Roderick P G Denman (who would lose his life in a Wellington in 1942) who sold it to Sweden in July 1936 where it became SE-AFE.

Armstrong Whitworth's first monoplane airliner was the AW.15 Atalanta of which eight were made between 1931 and 1932. G-ABTL, pictured here, was the penultimate example. Built exclusively for Imperial Airways' use on the Nairobi-Cape Town and Karachi-Singapore section of their long-distance runs to South Africa and Australia, they were products of the time when long journeys took not just many days but changes of aircraft types. The specification called for high cruising speed and sufficient reserve power to cater for 'hot and high' operations. Passenger space, today something of a foreign concept, was also thought worth mentioning. Remember this was still the time when flying-boats (which would be used for parts of the journey) still had observation decks! Power came from four Armstrong Siddeley Double Mongoose two-row radials now styled as Serval III. Named *Astraea*, this first flew in April 1933 and was eventually impressed by the Indian Air Force in March 1941 as DG450. It was withdrawn from use in September 1942. Nine passengers were carried in a spacious saloon.

At the other end of the scale, the four-seat DH.83 Fox Moth appeared early in 1932 to the design of Arthur Ernest Hagg. The prototype, G-ABUO pictured here at roll-out made its first flight that March before being shipped out to Canada for evaluation in the Canadian climate and also as a floatplane. This aircraft thus became CF-APL and its performance was so good that the DH factory at Toronto immediately put it into production. Meanwhile a total of 98 examples were put into production at Stag Lane. Enjoyed by all who flew in them, pilots and passengers, they were popular impressments and many saw service during the war years. After the war was over, DH Canada restarted production, some 52 being sold in that country. Canadian-built examples differed from British ones in that the interplane struts were of streamlined steel tube instead of spruce.

The single-engined Airspeed AS.5 Courier was an advanced aircraft at the time it was launched A H Tiltman's design first flew on April 10th, 1933. The third production aircraft was the green and gold G-ACLF fitted with a 277 hp Armstrong Siddeley Cheetah V engine which gave it a cruising speed of 152 mph. Designated the AS.5B, this was operated by R K Dundas until sale to North Eastern Airways at Croydon in March, 1937. It operated the Portsmouth – Ryde service for Portsmouth, Southsea & IOW Airways until the outbreak of war when it was impressed as X9342 and was dismantled at Kemble in 1943.

The Comper Swift was one of the bright lights of the early 1930s. A single-seat all-wood racer designed with structural lightness for speed, the diminutive folding-wing speedster was just what the racing pilot wanted! Flt Lt Nicholas Comper's friend was Douglas Rudolph Pobjoy, a pioneering radial-engine designer. He was developing a lightweight radial engine and Comper designed the Swift expressly for this motor. Delays in completing the engine and its certification meant that the prototype, G-AARX, was fitted with a 35 hp ABC Scorpion flat twin. The maiden flight was on May 17th, 1930. In fact, the first seven production models were powered by the 50 hp Salmson AD.9 radials. But then Rudolph Pobjoy was ready and he went on to develop the eponymous range of engines that powered many of the contemporary light aircraft. Here is a rare picture of a much-travelled Comper Swift, G-ACAG. Awarded its first C of A on November 16th, 1932, between 1933 and 1934 designer Comper flew it extensively around Europe on a sales tour. It was then sold to the Australian Aero Club (Victoria Section) and shipped as cargo on the SS *Ormonde* arriving at Melbourne on September 24th, 1934. Two weeks later it was test-flown at Essendon and on October 9th re-registered VH-UVC. It underwent several changes of ownership and numerous vicissitudes before ending up in New Zealand where, on November 7th, 2017, it was re-registered ZK-UVC to JEM Aviation at Omaka near Blenheim who undertook a sympathetic rebuild. On November 20th, 2017, it was test-flown at Omaka prior to transfer to Sydney – and another new registration. The Australians re-use letters as soon as they are relinquished and today's VH-UVC turns out to be a helicopter!

From the relatively lightweight, low-powered motor of the very first Comper Swift and with which the aircraft managed 100 mph, Nick Comper had the notion that a 120 hp DH Gipsy III ought to make it go even faster! The upshot was that this relatively huge engine was fitted. To keep the centre of gravity right, a whole forward fuselage structural bay was removed to fit the engine. The Gipsy Swift was indeed fast. While the Pobjoy Swift flew at 140 mph, Gipsy Swifts were no stranger to the 165 mph bracket. There were seven Gipsy Swifts built including one with the 130 hp Gipsy Major – the motor which powered the famed Tiger Moth. G-ABWW was flown at one time by Shuttleworth himself.

The Spartan Arrow G-ABWP was built in 1932. Its first registered owner was Richard Shuttleworth, the man after whom the renowned collection of vintage aircraft based at Old Warden is named. During the war it was stored and avoided impressment. After passing through several private owners post-war, 'BWP was purchased by Messers Ron Green, Bootle and Sweeting on March 15th, 1955. These enterprising enthusiasts formed themselves into The Spartan Flying Group and based their aircraft at Denham. The author was among the few allowed to fly this venerable old lady through the Buckinghamshire skies. Still flying today, the Arrow displays occasionally at Shuttleworth's air shows. Like their aircraft, the Spartan Flying Group also still exists at Denham, although today its current generation of members fly a Chipmunk.

Juan de la Cierva's problem, as far as the fellow directors of his company were concerned, was that he was continually improving his designs and that the company's goal of a 'production aircraft' seemed ever distant. True it was that numbers were built, but all too frequently the master would alter the machine. Not until the C.30 was a design 'finalised'. The C.19 was a case in point. It fulfilled all of its designed expectations. Then Cierva came up with the Mk.II which itself underwent three changes. Just when it seemed that here was a design to volume-produce and make money for the firm, Cierva made a further improvement. G-ABXG was a C.19 Mk.IIIP first flown at Hanworth on September 15th, 1932. This was the first to have a shaft-driven rotor to set it spinning for take-off. The previous C.19s had box tailplanes which directed the slipstream of the engine upwards to start the rotor on the ground. Now the machine had a single tail while the shaft to start the rotor can be seen just behind the front rotor pylon strut.

Nottingham's Experimental Light Plane Club was the creation of two lace-manufacturers, brothers Richard Francis Turney Granger and Richard John Turney Granger. Intrigued by the tailless designs created for Westland Aircraft by Captain Geoffrey Terence Roland Hill, they decided to design their own small tailless aircraft. With the help of Cecil Hugh Latimer-Needham of Luton Aircraft, they produced this novel one-off which they called the Granger Archaeopteryx. Registered G-ABXL and tested by pilot Charles Newham late in 1930, the machine flew astonishingly well behind a Douglas flat twin engine. It still exists, having been restored to flying condition by the Shuttleworth Trust at Old Warden.

Before the B A Swallow was the original 1927 German design, the Klemm L.25. It was Major Edward Freer Stephen of S T Lea Ltd who obtained the UK sales rights and it was he who imported the first models. Distinguishable from the subsequently British-built models, the original design had a rounded rudder and wing-tips plus external elevator and rudder cables that sprang from pulley wheels part way down the fuselage top decking. One of Stephen's imports was G-ABZO which, unlike most of the Klemm imports which were Salmson-powered, had a Pobjoy radial engine that drove an unusual four-blade wooden propeller. Described as an L.25C, 'BZO was sold on to Ireland becoming EI-ABJ, but did not survive a crash on August 13th, 1938.

Developed from the single-engined Courier, the Airspeed AS.6A Envoy Series I made its first appearance at the SBAC Show at Hendon on July 1st, 1934. The third AS.6A was G-ACVI *Miss Wolseley*. This was sold to Lord Nuffield at Castle Bromwich. Fitted with the new Wolseley Aries III engines, it was intended to take part in the MacRobertson Race to Australia but on the eve of the event, pilot George Lowdell damaged it in a forced landing at St Neots. Two years later it was sold to Ansett Airways Ltd as VH-UXM and embarked on a career that would amass to more than 10,000 flying hours. With spares for the Aries exhausted, it subsequently underwent a change to Wright Whirlwind engines in 1945. It was withdrawn from use in March 1951.

The Avro 619 Five, powered by three 105 hp Armstrong Siddeley Genet Major I radial engines, carried a pilot and four passengers and was a scaled down version of the Ten and a smaller Six. Designed by Roy Chadwick, it sold in the main to overseas airlines, and this one, VP-KAE with its early type windscreen, went straight from the Southampton to Wilson Airways Ltd at Nairobi in Kenya. Named *Knight of the Grail*, it unfortunately did not last long and, damaged in a crash, had to be replaced by Avro's demonstrator, G-AASO, which became VP-KAH. This one never got to bear these marks: flying still with its British letters, it crashed on January 18th, 1932, en route from Salisbury to Broken Hill. These big Avro monoplanes employed the Fokker wing technology for which Avro had purchased a licence. This concerned a one-piece plywood-covered wooden mainplane.

Another triple-engined mini-airliner was the Westland Wessex. Developed from the Westland IV of which two were made, eight Wessex were built, many of which went to Belgium and served SABENA. Among then was the third to be built, OO-AGE illustrated here. In March 1935 it returned to Britain, flying with Cobham Air Routes Ltd as G-ADEW on the Portsmouth-Christchurch-Guernsey route. On July 3rd, when flying over the Channel three miles south of The Needles, Isle of Wight, en route for Guernsey's L'Erée Aerodrome from Bournemouth,

the port engine failed. Pilot Robert William Henry Ogden continued on the remaining two engines but could not maintain height and was forced to ditch. The only passenger on board, Charles Frederick H Grainger, was picked up by the SS *Stanmore* and taken to Fowey in Cornwall but Ogden was never found. Unfortunately, the verdict was 'pilot error' although it was more likely to have been due to the age of the aircraft and its engines. The accident was the last straw for Cobham who, struggling operationally, sold his airline to Olley Air Service at Croydon.

Designed by William Stancliffe Shackleton and Cameron Lathrop Lee Murray, the Shackleton-Murray SM.1 two-seater was built for them by Airspeed Ltd at York. Based on the Curtiss-Wright Junior, this all-wood folding-wing aircraft was powered by a Hirth HM 60 four cylinder inverted in-line arranged as a pusher. The first flight was from Portsmouth in September 1933. Plans for production using the Pobjoy R radial were announced in May 1933, but came to nothing. The sole SM.1, registered G-ACBP in January 1935, was later sold to Lord Apsley of the Bristol and Wessex Aero Club. On July 22nd, 1936, His Lordship embarked on a flight from Yate, Gloucestershire, to Bembridge, Isle of Wight, but he came down in the sea off the Island after the engine failed. Apsley was rescued by a passing yacht and the aircraft was towed into Cowes Harbour. The wreck was stored for potential rebuild but plans were abandoned during the Second World War. It was delivered in March 1941 to an ATC Squadron at Stroud & District Technical College. Following an article in *The Aeroplane*, this unit wrote on November 14th, 1941, asserting their intention to rebuild the machine as a ground trainer with a Genet engine. The ultimate fate is unknown.

De Havilland's first real biplane airliner owed its existence to bus and air-taxi operator Edward Hillman who was very taken with the four-passenger Fox Moth. He asked if DH could build him a twin-engined variant. The upshot was the DH.84 Dragon which had outer wings based on those of the DH.83 with different tips and ailerons. Both wings were made to fold back outboard of the engine. First flown at Stag Lane on November 12th, 1932, the prototype was marked E.9 but afterwards as painted in Hillman's blue and white livery before delivery to Maylands Aerodrome in Essex. The Dragon was an immediate success and the type ultimately saw service all over the world. Besides those built at Edgware, they were also made in Canada and Australia. Here is one from 'down-under' – VH-AON which was built for the Royal Australian Air Force as A34-30. It carries the name *Puff*.

After some 63 Dragons had been built, Stag Lane introduced an improved version. Instead of the continuous windows of the original, as portrayed here, individually-framed windows were installed along the fuselage and the undercarriage struts were faired-in. The new variant was known as the Dragon 2. The DH.84 spearheaded de Havilland's famed group of biplanes which went on to produce the troublesome but elegant four-engined DH.86 Express, the DH.89 Dragon Rapide and the DH.90 Dragonfly which, while a biplane, an airliner and a twin-engined aircraft, was quite different from those that preceded it. Finally, and long forgotten in this roll-call, was the DH.92 Dolphin, DH's only biplane with a retractable undercarriage. The picture shows Dragon 1 VH-AON photographed at the Antique Aircraft Association of Australia's fly-in at Clare Valley Aerodrome in October 2019. *Picture by Andrew Lesty via Tony Campbell*

Avro built many variants of its Cadet biplane trainer. Dating from 1933, the Avro 638 Club Cadet was introduced for flying clubs and private owners. A number were made, the Airwork School at Heston taking three all powered by the 130 hp Gipsy Major I. The last of these was G-ACHP which got its C of A on June 26th, 1933. During the war this was impressed to Saunders-Roe Ltd as HM570 as a replacement for the Spartan Clipper G-ACEG destroyed in a raid on Somerton Airport. The Cadet emerged at the end of war unscathed and was acquired by the Vintage Aeroplane Club at Denham. On January 1st, 1956, a Handley Page air test observer from the Victor V-bomber line, Jock Ogilvy, decided to take his friend G H Cullen for a flight in the Cadet. He was warned that there was a line-squall expected to come through around mid-day. He took off at 12.10 hrs and immediately hit extreme turbulence which directed him into the woods on the north-east corner of the airfield. The Cadet struck two tree-tops and was wrecked beyond repair. Neither occupant was hurt but the type became extinct as a result.

After the success of the Swift, Comper designed three more light aircraft – the single-seat Streak, the two-seat Kite and the advanced three-seat Mouse with retractable undercarriage, seen here. The first flight of the Mouse took place of September 11th, 1933, in the hands of designer Nicholas Comper, but it was a further five months and after trials at A & A E E Martlesham Heath which initiated a few minor airframe changes before the C of A was issued on May 22nd, 1934. During this whole time the aircraft bore no markings and was only finished in red oxide primer dope. Now registered G-ACIX, the Heston-built Gipsy Major-powered monoplane featured a three-stage sliding cockpit hood: a novelty at the time.

Officially owned by Comper Aircraft Ltd director Sir Norman J Watson, the Mouse was built for racing and on July 12th and 13th, 1934, it was flown by Flt.Lt E H Newman in heats for the King's Cup Race at Hatfield Aerodrome. Poor weather prevailed and the Mouse was out in the first heat. It had, however, managed a useful average of speed of 132.75 mph. In what was already a competitive market for touring aircraft, the Mouse failed to attract the hoped-for sales, and only this one was completed before the Comper company was wound up in August 1934 to be replaced by Heston Aircraft Ltd founded on August 10th.

Comper's Streak racer was a single-seat low-wing version of the Swift and the Kite, pictured here, a tandem two-seat variant of the Streak. Like the earlier Mouse, the undercarriage was retractable and fitted with wheel-brakes. Although registered G-ACME, the Kite was to spend its life in red primer and only got around to displaying its letters just before the King's Cup Race. With its 90 hp Pobjoy Niagara engine, the Kite fuselage was not unlike that of the Swift but the second cockpit was created by inserting an extra bay. This, the last aircraft to be completed by the Comper company, flew early in the summer of 1934, only a month after the Streak, and gained its C of A on July 10th. With the front cockpit faired over, it flew in the 1934 King's Cup Race at an average speed of 144 mph but was eliminated in the heats because the undercarriage could not be retracted. The Kite was never tried in the tourer role for which it was designed, and its development was overtaken by the closure of the Comper business in August 1934. Taken over by newly-formed Heston Aircraft, the new firm had no interest in the Kite. Along with all the other company machines in the Heston hangar, they were broken up and burned in 1935.

Intended for participation in the Coupé Deutsch Race staged at Étampes on May 27th, 1934, Nicholas Comper's single-seat Streak was a low-wing variant of the Swift fitted with a high-compression Gipsy Major engine which could develop 146 hp. Registered G-ACNC, the benefits of a retractable undercarriage were expected to give the Streak a top speed of close to 200 mph. In effect Comper was unable to complete the Étampes race due to undercarriage problems.

Comper shifted his sights to the 1934 King's Cup Race and, after averaging 175.5 mph, the Streak was forced to abandon that race at Wittering. The closure of Comper's Heston workshop saw the Streak pass into the hands of Philip de Walden Avery who took the Streak to the following year's King's Cup Race. In this he averaged 173.5 mph but even so was unplaced. Two years later the Streak was the last of Comper's line-up of unique aircraft to be broken up at Heston.

Imperial Airways was greatly impressed by the performance of the four-engined Short S.17 flying-boat and it believed that these benefits might also extend to a land version. The upshot was the curiously top-heavy-looking Short L.17, two of which were built using Kent superstructures and square-sectioned fuselages to provide maximum space. The two aircraft were G-ACJJ *Scylla*, pictured here by the hangars at Croydon, and her sister model G-ACJK *Syrinx*. Each could carry 39 passengers and was powered by four 595 hp Bristol Jupiter XFBM radial engines. Built at Rochester, they entered service in 1934. Each met its fate in 1940 – blown over in a gale. Airline publicity of the time tells us they each had 'two mail and freight holds, a kitchen and two lavatories' and a fully loaded weight of 'over 14 tons'.

Before the British Aircraft (BA) Swallow and a name-change, the company formed at Hanworth was called British Klemm (BK) and this firm copied the original German design. The BK.1 Swallow was officially the L.25C 1A and six were built before company designer George H Handasyde and test pilot Edmund G Hordern revised it to the fine flying, but angular-looking, BA Swallow. The very first product was this, the Salmson AD.9-powered BK.1, G-ACMK, first flown in December 1933. This survived the war and was sold to Ireland in March 1948 where it became EI-ADS owned and operated by Weston Air Services. It was withdrawn from service in June 1960 and was broken up some years later.

Kenneth Noble Pearson believed ailerons were the wrong shape and that they ought to be shaped more like a dustbin lid. He tried them out on Col G L P Henderson's Avro 548 G-EBAJ before making a feature of them on the Glenny & Henderson Gadfly. They worked – after a fashion. Significantly, the rotary-aileroned Gadfly was quickly retro-fitted with conventional ailerons after 'proving flights'. This was in the autumn of 1929 at Brooklands. But Pearson was not yet finished! The appearance at Hanworth in December 1933 of a curious pusher monoplane without any form of vertical tail caused some raised eyebrows.

The work of K N Pearson and C L Pickering together with D Horsfield, the so-called Pickering/Pearson KP.2, G-ACMR, appeared to herald an aerodynamic advance of world-changing capabilities. With its elderly 26 hp Aeronca E-107 flat twin engine mounted atop the wing as a pusher, the KP.2 charged around Hanworth Aerodrome in circles, quite incapable of maintaining anything like a straight line. Rotary ailerons or not, the KP.2 (with coy, but unexplained, implications of there having been a predecessor) did not fly. The later addition of a small fin proved ineffective. G-ACMR probably never displayed its letters. It was scrapped in 1935.

Airspeed's AS.5 all-wood six-seat Courier is remembered as being the first aircraft with a retractable undercarriage to go into production. Worked hydraulically by hand-pump, this mechanism increased cruising speed by 13 mph for a weight penalty of only 30 lbs. The first one was built at York for Sir Alan Cobham's planned flight to India which would pioneer long-distance flight-refuelling. When the company moved to Portsmouth, this was taken by road for completion. Pictured here is the seventh aircraft to be built, G-ACNZ of June 1934 and fitted experimentally with the 324 hp Napier Rapier 'H'-shaped engine driving a four-blade propeller (a pair of superimposed two-bladers). After trials it was re-engined with the standard AS Lynx IVC and sold to Portsmouth, Southsea & Isle of Wight Aviation Ltd for use on the Portsmouth-Ryde run. Impressed as X9346 in March 1940, it was struck off charge and scrapped at Kemble in April 1944.

The Airspeed AS.6 Envoy was the precursor of the Viceroy, the wartime Oxford and post-war Consul. In turn it was a development of the single-engined Airspeed Courier of 1934. Here is a fine air-to-air view of the prototype Envoy. The silver and green prototype G-ACMT had been premiered at the Hendon SBAC Show on July 1st that year where it had created quite a stir for its modern lines. This picture was taken on April 2nd, 1936, and shows the Envoy after it had been converted to a Series II with flaps and more powerful engines – 220 hp Armstrong Siddeley Lynx IVC radials. Here in this fine picture of Neville Shute Norway and Alfred Hessell Tiltman's creation they are seen over-flying the *Queen Mary* in Cowes roads.

There was something rather childish in the shape of Edgar Percival's first Mew Gull. As related in the book *Percival Aircraft: Edgar Percival, the Man and his Legacy* (Stenlake, 2013), Percival's prototype was not particularly streamlined but, thanks first to Roland Bound and then Arthur Bage who redesigned it and came out with an entirely different profile, it became a first-rate racer. After Jack Cross of Essex Aero super-refined it, the Mew Gull topped 247 mph. Percival was no aerodynamicist whereas Bage was. Although Percival petulantly went through life claiming that the racing Mew Gull was entirely his – and only his – design, Percival's valuable contribution was to finance its construction. This picture was taken at Gravesend on March 15th, 1934 – the occasion being Percival, flying in his trade-mark trilby hat, showing off his creation to the press. But it was Bage's revamped Mew Gull, also registered G-ACND, that participated in the record-breaking flights. Alex Henshaw set up an astonishing out-and-back Cape record in February 1939 in what is today the only survivor of the six built – G-AEXF. It is still flying today after many crashes and sympathetic rebuilds.

When DH-60G-III Moth Major G-ADHE crashed at Rickmansworth in March 1958, many mourned the passing of the last of its type remaining in Britain. However, at the time they were built, a good proportion were exported. The type was remembered as the first to be built with an inverted engine. The example illustrated here, G-ACNS, got its C of A on February 16th, 1934, and stayed in Britain until March of 1940 when brokers W S Shackleton sold her to South Africa where she became ZS-ARW. In recent years the aircraft has been repatriated as have a few others predominantly from Australia. As of 2018 there were six Moth Majors back on the UK register, all having retrieved their original UK markings.

Many confuse the autogyro with the helicopter: the latter has an engine-driven rotor which, because it is powered, generates torque which will turn the fuselage in the opposite direction, hence the need for the helicopter's tail rotor to counteract this spinning force. With the autogyro the rotor may indeed be powered to set it in rotation, but then the power must be disengaged and it becomes the slipstream that keeps the rotor turning. Originally the rotor was spun up by men pulling on a rope round a hub-pulley. Rotor speed and power can also be regulated by altering the pitch of the blades and this is a key feature of the helicopter. One autogiro, the Kay Gyroplane, pioneered this blade incidence control on the autogiro's free rotor. Designed by a Scotsman, David Kay, aided by John Grieve of Scone, the first machine was the 32/1 built for Kay by a local Perth garage and flown at Leuchars that year. The second, pictured here, was the 33/1. Built by Cierva's rotor makers, Oddie, Bradbury & Cull of Southampton, and powered by a 75 hp Pobjoy, it was test-flown at Eastleigh in 1935. It was at one time the smallest and fastest autogyro of its time. Its star quality was that it pioneered collective-pitch control – core of the helicopter rotor. Kay was clearly a genius but he ran out of finance and his work (and patents) went for others to exploit. The Gyroplane, G-ACVA, is preserved in Scotland's Museum of Flight. David Kay did more than many others to diminish that gap between the autogiro and the helicopter and should not be forgotten.

The prototype DH.87 Hornet Moth, marked E.6 and later registered G-ACTA, started out in 1934 as an experimental design in the quest for an updated replacement for the Gipsy Moth. It first flew at Hatfield on May 9th, 1934, and then went straight off to compete in the King's Cup Race on July 13th. While averaging 127 mph in the heats, it was eliminated. Note the rounded wing-tips, the cause of the majority of early problems with the type. Wings with a much greater taper were tried but these made the handling characteristics worse, the aircraft flicking into a stall with less warning. Tapered-wing Hornet Moths were known as DH.87A, and now trials began with what would be found as the ideal wing shape – the almost square-tipped rectangular profile of the popular DH.87B. Here we see the prototype shortly before its first flight. It was scrapped at Hatfield in February 1946.

It is a sobering thought that the DH.84 Dragon was such a marketing success for de Havilland. In total, 115 were made initially at Stag Lane and latterly at Hatfield. Pictured here is G-ACOR *Fiona*, a Dragon Mk.II which was the refined version of the Mk.I dating from September 1936. This aircraft served with British Colonial Airways at Croydon and then went to British Airways Ltd at Gatwick in March, 1937. It operated with Northern & Scottish Airways Ltd at Renfrew before going to Australia in February 1938 where it became VH-AEA. Then with Australian airline pioneer Raymond John Paul Parer (1894 –1967) at Wewak, Papua, New Guinea. Subsequently it was damaged by enemy action at Salamaua on January 21st, 1942, and was abandoned. *Photograph by Charles E Brown.*

The DH.86 was a bold statement for its makers yet one which Sir Geoffrey de Havilland chose to forget in his autobiography. The big four-engined biplane would turn out to be something of a wayward child. When DH's engine genius, Major Frank Halford, produced his six-cylinder version of the Gipsy Major, so creating the 200 hp Gipsy Six, it coincided with the Australian Government issuing a specification for a fast multi-engined mail and passenger aircraft to operate the last leg of the Imperial Airways' England-Australia service which required crossing the Java and Timor seas. G-ACPL (E.2) was the prototype of

the nameless ten-seater DH.86. It was created in just four months from drawing-board to completion making its first flight at Stag Lane on January 14th, 1934 piloted by Hubert Stanford Broad. With two others (G-ACVY and 'CVZ), trials took place with Railway Air Services Ltd who named G-ACPL *Delphinus*. These three, plus a fourth registered VH-URN, had a single pilot cockpit in the nose as in the Dragon and, later, in the DH.89 Rapide.

The DH.86 was a grand aircraft to fly and, with its singing bracing wires and four Gipsy engines, produced a memorable sound. But the Australians were not satisfied, urging an increase in fuel capacity to 183 gallons for long-haul operation, plus the need to have two pilots side-by-side. The first two-pilot DH.86 to be built was G-ACWC named *Delia* for Imperial Airways Ltd. The nose was totally restructured to make it wide enough for a pair of pilots seated side by side with revised glazing for front, sides and cabin top. This new nose added two feet two inches to the aircraft's overall length. Of the four single-seat models made, G-ACPL was rebuilt for two crew but G-ACVY *Mercury* and 'CVZ *Jupiter* were left as singles for Railway Air Services. The former was written off in a night-time crash at Cologne in March 1937, and the latter was broken up at Langley in 1948. The second machine, VH-URN *Miss Hobart*, took Australian airline founder Victor Holyman and his ten passengers to their deaths in a ditching in the Bass Strait in October, 1934.

A modified DH.86 version was introduced in late 1935. This, the DH.86A, had pneumatic undercarriage legs, improved wheel brakes and tail-wheel plus a shallower windscreen angle. It was offered with Gipsy Six I engines driving either wooden airscrews or Fairey-Reed metal propellers. An option was the Gipsy Six Series II engines: only one was flown in this form and that reverted to Series I engines before sale. Some problems persisted in handling and the upshot was the DH-86B, pictured here. This had increased tailplane chord at the tips plus 'Zulu-shield' auxiliary fins to the ends of the tailplane. The aileron gearing was also revised to minimise pilot force needed for full movement. The first DH.86B was G-AENR, pictured here. This was tested at Martlesham Heath in February 1937 and went on to serve Blackpool & West Coast Air Services Ltd. It was reduced to produce at Langley in 1948. In all there were four single-crew DH.86 built, 29 two-crew DH.86, 20 DH.86A (all converted to DH.86B in 1937), and 10 DH.86B. The type is now extinct.

One of the DH.86A aircraft converted into a DH.86B was Imperial Airways' G-ADUH *Dryad* which they took delivery of in March of 1936. Two years later in October it went to Aer Lingus as EI-ABT *Sasana* and was based at Dublin's Baldonnel Aerodrome where this picture was taken in 1939. In November 1946 it came back on the UK register as G-ADUH and was operated by Gulf Aviation Ltd in May 1951. The following month it was written off in a ground collision with Auster J-1 G-AIBO at Bahrain. The DH.86B was unofficially (but widely) called the Express – a name which de Havilland would not acknowledge.

Late in 1933, de Havilland sought a faster and more comfortable version of its Hillman-inspired Dragon airliner. The upshot was a scaled-down twin-engined version of the DH.86. Designated the DH.89 it was powered by two Gipsy Six engines and, largely because of this, its first name was the Dragon Six. By the time production began this had been altered to Dragon Rapide. Over the years the name had been almost universally reduced to Rapide. The prototype first flew at Hatfield on April 17th, 1934. Rapides were immensely influential in the development of air services, especially the small routes. As well as the civilian market, many were built to Service contracts where the RAF called them Dominies. The introduction of landing flaps produced the designation DH.89A. Pictured here from March, 1937, is one of these, G-AERN, when it was operated first by Blackpool & West Coast Air Services Ltd, and later by Olley. Sold to Spain in January 1954, it became EC-AKO.

Although the DH.90 looks like an evolutionary step in the biplane airliner that had begun with the Dragon and moved on through Rapide, the Dragonfly was a very different aircraft having a plywood monocoque fuselage. Intended as a five-seat luxury tourer, it was the 'business jet' of the mid-1930s. The prototype G-ADNA (E.2) first flew at Hatfield on August 12th 1935 and this was the first of 66 production models to emerge from Hatfield. Gipsy Major I engines (later IC and 10 versions) provided power. G-AEDU, seen here, has an interesting registration history. This registration was never actually taken up. While allocated, the original aircraft was registered G-ADXM. The unissued allocation was delivered to Angola in 1937 where it flew as CR-AAB and, later, as ZS-CTR in South Africa. When it came back to England in 1979 it took up its allocated but never used letters – G-AEDU. Exported to America in 1983 as N190DH, it had a bad crash and was acquired by Sir Torquil Patrick Alexander Norman (1933-) who brought it back to the UK in 1992 in small pieces: he is alleged to have 'carried it home in Tesco plastic bags'! It was rebuilt to flying condition and one more bore the letters G-AEDU.

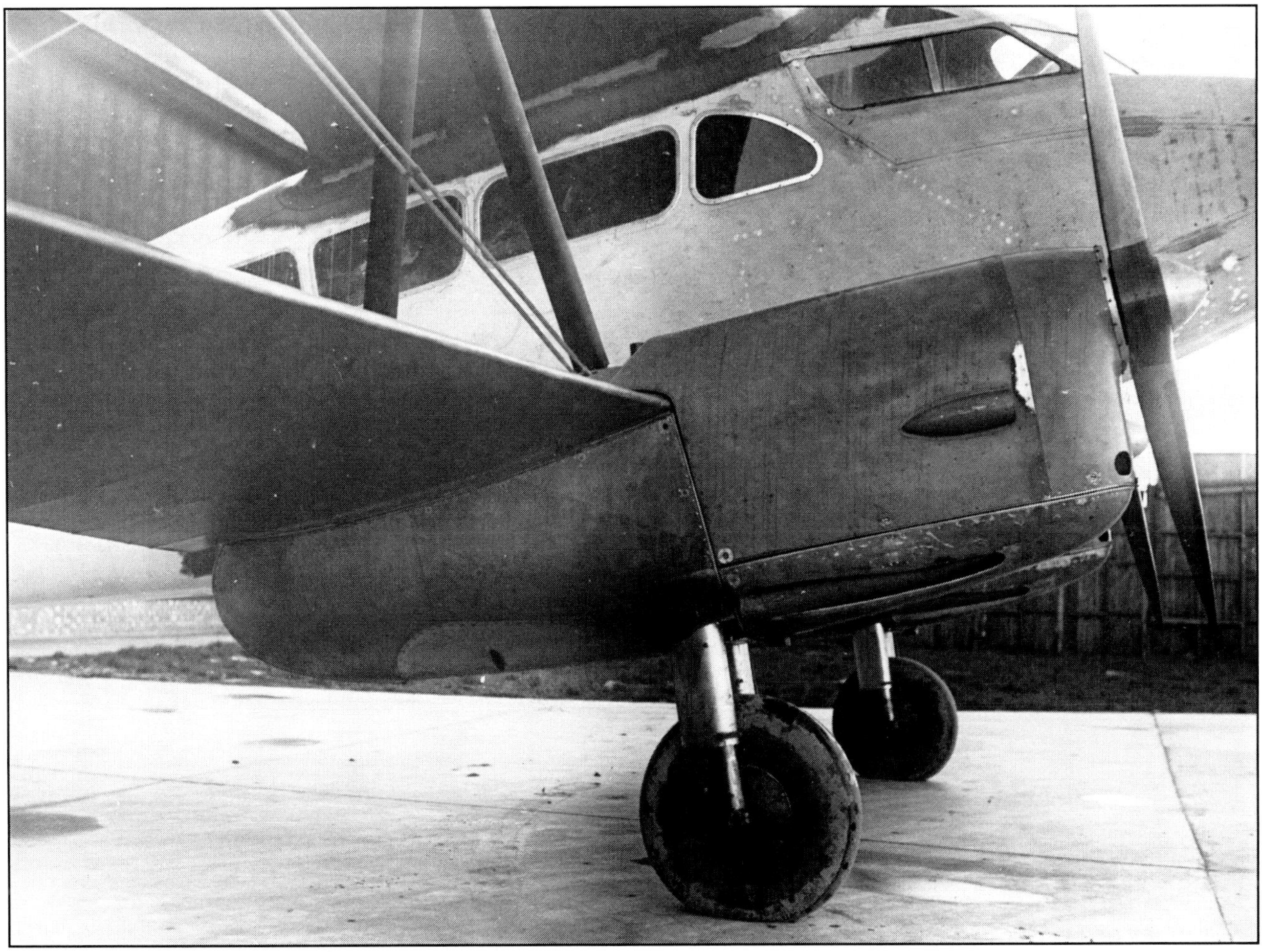

Last of the DH biplanes was the DH.92 Dolphin. Based on the Rapide but with a slightly greater wing-span, the Dolphin had a two-pilot cockpit like the DH.86. Its major change, however, was the undercarriage which was retractable. Powered by two 204 hp Gipsy Six Series II engines driving constant-speed propellers, only one was built – G-AEMX. Flown at Hatfield in August of 1936, it was structurally too heavy and the performance benefits of the foldable wheels insufficient. It was scrapped two months later and is remembered as the only DH type never to have been photographed save for a few pictures, like this one, of the undercarriage. It is believed never to have carried its registration letters.

Miles Aircraft made some of the most attractive low-wing monoplanes of the inter-war period. None was more successful than the Hawk series. The designation M.2 would cover models from the plain M.2 of October 1932 through the M.2A and eventually the M.2Y. Some of these were sole examples: others, like the M.2F Hawk Major, pictured here, entered production. In this case, 16 would be built of which G-ACYO, the 12th to be constructed, had a particularly interesting life. Registered on September 24th 1934 to John Myles Bickerton, founder of Hawksridge Aerodrome, later renamed Denham, it was initially kept at Hanworth where it was stored on the outbreak of war until impressed in 1943 as NF752. Restored to Reading Aero Club, it was later the property of ex-ATA pilot Miss Freydis Leaf who became British Air Racing Champion in 1954 flying this aircraft. It was then sold to Frederick Howard Stirling who crashed it at Elstree on November 28th, 1954. He allegedly stalled on take-off. He survived: the Hawk didn't.

G-ADCV was a Miles M.2M Hawk Major three-seater registered on February 20th, 1935 to John Eric Duncan Holder who kept it at Heston. After wartime storage it was restored to racing pilot Ronald Royal Paine of Weybridge. After several more changes of ownership it ended up in the hands of Basil Henry St Andrew Hurle-Hobbs who stored it in the open at Croydon where, on February 4th, 1950, a gale blew a wall onto it, crushing the life out of the poor thing.

The Hawk formula continued for many years undergoing progressive development. The last came in 1938 with the M.17 Monarch of which eleven would be built. G-AFJU was the third made at Woodley by Phillips & Powis. This was the first Miles product to be designed entirely by George H Miles, F G's younger brother. A step up from the M.11A Whitney Straight, the Monarch was the last to emerge from Woodley before the war. First flown on February 21st, 1938, by chief test pilot Harold William Chetwynd 'Bill' Skinner (1903-1939), the aircraft's real success came after the conflict when sporting pilots such as W P Bowles raced the aircraft into first place in the 1957 Goodyear Trophy, third place in the 1958 King's Cup and first in that year's Norton Griffiths Trophy. G-AFJU had ten post-war owners including the Cotswold Aero Club. It was eventually scrapped in 1964 at Staverton.

The M.5 Sparrowhawk was expressly designed for F G Miles' participation in the 1935 King's Cup Race. A single-seater, it was built from standard M.2 Hawk components but with shorter fuselage, lower top decking and the seat reduced to a bottom-skin bum-rest with the mainspar passing under the pilot's knees. The centre-section was reduced to fuselage width so cutting five feet off the span while the undercarriage track was increased. A high-compression Gipsy Major generated 147 hp up front. While winning the average speed prize it only made 11th in the final. The following year it made ninth and seventh in 1937. Pictured here is G-AELT which Victor Smith flew in the 1936 Schlesinger Race from Portsmouth to Johannesburg. Smith retired at Cairo with oil problems and sold his mount which became ZS-ANO with a cabin-top. The poor Sparrowhawk was an elegant disappointment.

When Heston Aircraft acquired the assets of Comper Aircraft Ltd, a successor to the small racers might have been expected. Instead what emerged from the hangar was this sleek five-seat executive aircraft with the novelty and luxury of a Dowty hydraulically-operated retractable undercarriage. George Cornwall's all-wood design folded its wheels into thickened fairings from which sprang the wing's lift-struts. It was truly revolutionary. The prototype, G-ADAD seen here, was first flown on August 18th 1935 flown by Edmund Gwyn Hordern and proved to be 7 mph faster than its design speed cruising at 125 mph on its 200 hp Gipsy Six engine. Six aircraft were built five, of which remained in Britain.

The sole Heston Phoenix made for an overseas buyer was Australian racing pilot Charles James 'Jimmy' Melrose's VH-AJM. Melrose (1913-1936) flew the aircraft from Heston to Australia where, in July 1936, he and a passenger were killed when the Phoenix broke up in turbulence over South Melton, Victoria on a charter flight from Melbourne to Darwin. He was just 22 years old. The last surviving Phoenix, G-AESV, saw out its final years as the property of Arthur Robert 'Tiny' Pilgrim at Elstree. It eventually ran out of luck when, in April 1952, oil-pressure failure forced an emergency landing on an inaccessible place in the French Alps. The aircraft was only slightly damaged but its location meant that it could not be repatriated. In accordance with mountain-rescue rules, it was burned where it stood. Pilgrim, meanwhile, managed to salvage the engine.

The Short S.16 Scion twin-engined cantilever monoplane was designed by Arthur Gouge for feeder-line work and was first shown at the 1934 SBAC Show at Hendon. A five-seater plus pilot, the Scion had a welded tubular steel fuselage and a fabric-covered metal-framed wing. Pobjoy radial-powered, five of the five-seater Mark 1 models were made before a general cleaning-up of the design, best seen in the re-alignment of all the fuselage windows and the raising of the engine thrust-lines to the wing leading edge. This became the six-seat Mark 2 of which Short Brothers built ten and Pobjoy an extra four. G-ADDN, seen here was the second made and was impressed as X9364 and struck off charge in November 1941.

The last Short Scion Mk.2 was also the last survivor of the type. Pobjoy-built and first flown as a seaplane on December 9th, 1937, it flew at Freetown, Sierra Leone, for a brief while before being returned to Rochester where it was converted back to a standard landplane in November of 1941 for operation by Air Couriers under the markings M-5 at Barton-in-the-Clay. Post war it went to Air Couriers at Gatwick where it underwent an extensive refurbishment. Despite grand plans for expansion, this company, formed at Croydon in 1938, did not last and G-AEZF was turfed out of its hangar for open storage in May 1950. Flown to Redhill in good, restorable condition with its blue upholstered interior in fine shape, there were fresh hopes but over the years it gradually deteriorated. Half a century later its remains are being venerated – but its flying days are but a memory.

The DH.60 Moth came in a variety of styles including with upright engines (Gipsy I and II, Cirrus Hermes) and inverted (Gipsy III). The early ones had a through-axle landing gear and later models the divided undercarriage of the later Tiger Moth. A popular model was the DH.60GIII also known as the Moth Major. As related earlier, of the large number built, most were for export and only 28 appeared on the British register. Post war, only this one, G-ADHE operated by Percy Hindmarsh's Vintage Aeroplane Club, was left. Based at Denham it was often flown by Cyril Mills, son of circus proprietor Bertram Mills. The type faced extinction when, on March 22nd, 1958, G-ADHE crashed at Shepherds Lane, Mills End, Rickmansworth. Later repatriations have seen the type back in our skies.

The BAC Drone powered glider was the brainchild of Charles Herbert Lowe-Wylde from Maidstone, Kent. While he himself did not live to see the full achievements of his creation (he suffered an incapacitation in flight and was killed in an early version of his machine), the Drone went on to amuse and amaze several generations of pilots. This example, G-ADPJ, was a historic machine. On March 26th, 1936, Col the Master of Sempill (William Francis Forbes-Sempill [1893-1965]) flew this 23 hp Douglas Sprite-powered Drone II some 570 miles from Croydon to Berlin Tempelhof Airport in 11 hours. He returned a few days later in 9 hours though he interrupted the flight with a stop at Canterbury, Kent. The Drone had consumed just £1.5/- worth of petrol. Post war this Drone, with its owner Albert C Waterhouse, was one of the pioneer fighters for the rebirth of the Permit to Fly system. Unfortunately it was completely flattened by the collapse of a heavy hangar door onto it in a gale. Rebuilt, it enjoyed eight years of flight until on April 3rd, 1955, engine failure on take-off from Leicester East ended badly: it finished up upside down with Waterhouse hanging in his straps soaked in petrol and with serious back injuries. Recent rebuild attempts are still ongoing.

G-AEKV was another BAC Drone dating from September 1936, the fourth from last to be made at Hanworth by the newly-named Kronfeld Ltd. This one was of a style named the Drone de Luxe and was powered by a 30 hp Carden-Ford water-cooled motorcar engine as converted by enthusiast Sir John Valentine Carden. This high-revving motor gave 'EKV a distinctive sound rather like a mosquito of the biting type. After a good career of flying post-war it is today in the collection of Brooklands Museum in Surrey. On one occasion, a burst radiator pipe deposited a large quantity of very hot water down the author's neck necessitating a forced landing and a plethora of dubious language.

Blackburn's B-2 was a trainer based on the Gipsy-powered Bluebird. There was something about the appearance of this gangly biplane with its Alclad-covered fuselage, wide-gapped unstaggered and unswept wings and curious centre-section strutting that emphasised the genius behind de Havilland's Tiger Moth. No, the B-2 was an acquired taste and its appearance was not helped by the 'clutching-hand' wing slots. The prototype made its first public appearance at the Hendon SBAC Show on June 27th, 1932. The following week it took part in the King's Cup Race but only managed an 18th place finish. Used at Hanworth for training in the 'thirties, the B-2 was a poor second to the Moth. Of the 42 built, a disproportionate number were lost in accidents ranging from flying mishaps to unforeseen events on the ground. After the war, two were left – G-ACLD and this one, G-AEBJ. The former stalled on a low-level turn at a York airshow in June 1952. This one is the last of the breed and, like the Hatfield Moth, is lovingly preserved by its makers.

The BA Swallow was the British designed and built version of the original German Klemm design. Much as the original had a lot going for it, the more angular British version produced at Hanworth possessed both a certain charm and a surprisingly good performance. While the first British Klemm Swallows (22 built on the British register) were 75 hp Salmson radial-powered, BA's products were split between 90 hp Pobjoy radial-powered (43 built) and 90 hp Cirrus Minor inline-powered (47 made). Here is a fine profile of a Pobjoy-powered model, the light blue and silver G-ADPS.

G-AEMW was the sole example of a BA Swallow Mk 2 which had been converted to a neat cabin top. First registered in September 1936, it performed yeoman service in Scotland before the war. It escaped impressment and was lovingly restored at Perth in 1946 before being transferred first to Broxbourne and then to Elstree where it lived for many years. On December 29th, 1963, landing back at a private airstrip at Clothall Common, Baldock, Hertfordshire, the aircraft stalled into the ground and nosed over onto its back. No more Echo Mike Whiskey.

The mid-1930s saw the start of the Pou-du-Ciel craze in Britain. Frenchman Henri Mignet's tiny aircraft was best described as a super-staggered tailless biplane and its designer, a radio engineer whose aviation and aircraft design experience was entirely of the self-taught, deductive type, held no qualifications besides boundless enthusiasm. Having taken his own country by storm and inspired countless budding flyers to start building their own aircraft, he thought he would infect Britain with his Flea culture. On August 13th, 1935, he set off from Saint-Inglevert in his HM-14 to cross La Manche to Lympne. We Brits got wind of his invasion and he was escorted by a Cierva C.30A G-ACYC and a DH Dragon full of press photographers from Croydon. Here is one of their pictures. On August 17th, Mignet demonstrated his Flying Flea (as we called it over here) at Shoreham. Incidentally, the Autogiro belonged to Henly's at Heston and they later sold it in France as F-AOHZ.

Built at Staplehill, Bristol in 1936 by Henry James 'Harry' Dolman was G-AEHM, an HM-14 Flying Flea. He named it *Blue Finch*. It is seen here in its early form with a two-cylinder upright motorcycle engine. The Flea was underpowered with this motor so after an early crash it was rebuilt with a 35 hp ABC Scorpion flat twin. In this state it was exhibited at the *Daily Mail* 50 Years of Flying Exhibition at Hendon in July 1951. It is preserved in the Science Museum Collection.

One of the better-known home-built Fleas was G-ADXS built at Southend by Chris L Storey, proprietor of the Alexander Street garage. Fitted with a 25 hp Scott Flying Squirrel engine, and named *The Fleeing Fly*, Storey used it in many promotional activities, mostly associated with trucking it around his home-town standing in the rear of a lorry. It did fly, briefly, at Southend Airport on January 20th, 1936, and was resurrected as a garage attraction after the war before going into a Southend museum, now disbanded. The Flea still exists.

The sole example of the all-metal Pobjoy-powered CLW Curlew two-seater, G-ADYU, was built to prove a single-spar duralumin wing design evolved by Francis Welham and Arthur Levell. This comprised a cross-braced spar box bearing cantilever wing ribs. It was, claimed the designers, both strong for its weight and cost. With financial support from Stanton Wilding Cole of the EKCO radio company, Welham and Levell set up a company known by their initials as CLW Aviation, based at Gravesend, Kent, and built a wing for testing. This performed better than estimated and inspired the men to create an aircraft to evaluate it. Proposed as a possible aircraft for the private owner as well as the trainer market, it made its first flight at Gravesend on September 3rd, 1936, in the hands of former Beardmore pilot Archibald Norman Kingwill. Despite proving itself an above-average flyer, and although on test it was successfully dived at an astonishing 305 mph, its makers were underfunded and the business bankrupt. G-ADYU went first to Essex Aero Ltd, then to Martlesham Heath, gaining its C of A on November 19th, 1936. It appears to have done little flying after that, being put up for sale in July 1938. Stored during the war, it was broken up in 1948.

Unusual aeroplanes are nothing new, neither are those apparently so coy that their very existence seems improbable. So it was with G-AECN, the Burgoyne-Stirling Dicer, also sometimes known as the Darley Monoplane. Doubts over sanity arise when it is found that G-AECN was a Flying Flea! Donovan Cookes Burgoyne (1901-1980) was a talented aircraft carpenter despite having lost his right hand in childhood. In 1936 he began a Flying Flea and registered it G-AECN. By the time it was finished, Fleas in Britain were grounded, so he built a single seat monoplane at his Darley Green, Warwickshire, home. Originally he called it the Darley Monoplane. It was made using the cut-down fuselage of a BK Swallow with wings from the same source cut down and shortened. During the war the unfinished airframe stood engineless at Don's new home, Heronfield Farm, close to Knowle Airfield. Here Burgoyne rebuilt training gliders for the RAF during the war. During 1946, F/O Frederick Howard Stirling (1891–1957) acquired the airframe and fitted it with an American-made Aeronca E.113C engine. At the same time, he 'borrowed' that unused Flea registration. A number of successful flights ensued including one to RAF Wymeswold. The total illegality of the aircraft mitigated against further success and, despite its promising flights, it 'disappeared'. It is pictured here at Honiley on August 28th, 1948.

Basil Balfour Henderson was one of the better designers of the inter-war years. Besides an unfortunate involvement with Edgar Percival, his work was respected enough by MP, ace aviator and racing motorist Whitney Willard Straight for him to commission the design of an aircraft offering both comfort and the joint racing attributes of high cruising speed along with a very low landing speed. Construction of the prototype Hendy 3308 Heck was undertaken by Westland Aircraft Works at Yeovil. Registered G-ACTC, it first flew in July 1934. This aircraft had a retractable landing gear. Parnall Aircraft Limited was formed in May 1935 when George Parnall & Co merged with the Hendy Aircraft Co and the armament engineering firm Nash & Thompson Ltd. Redesignated the Parnall Heck, a number of problems with the undercarriage led to it being locked down and fitted with fairings and wheel spats. The aircraft set a new record for the flight from Cape Town to England of 6 days, 8 hours and 27 minutes in November 1936. With the prototype, only eight aircraft were made and none was sold. Here G-AEGH poses at Yate in 1938. Impressed as NF749, it was scrapped at Kemble in May 1944.

The first British aircraft to be constructed in metal using drop-presses, the CW Cygnet appeared in 1936, the brainchild of Carl Robert Chronander (1910-2002) and James Ivor Waddington (1910-1992). The two men set up a small factory on the Slough Trading Estate but very soon ran out of money. Talks had been progressing with the General Aircraft Company now at Hanworth. The designers had contemplated selling production aircraft for £800. After the design rights were acquired from General Aircraft, a certain amount of redesign took place, including the substitution of the 90 hp Cirrus Minor. Price was now £895 but the design scored on ease of production. The outbreak of war ended the project after just eight were built plus the prototype CW design, G-AEMA, seen here coming in to land with flaps down.

The Percival Vega Gull four-seater tourer was the precursor of the Percival Proctor. It was derived from the earlier 'D-Series' Gull three-seater. Designed by the talented designer Arthur Bage and built at Gravesend by Percival Aircraft Ltd, the primary differences between this and the earlier design were the provision of an additional fourth seat, dual controls and flaps. The fuselage was also wider and the wing-span increased. The prototype G-AEAB first flew from Gravesend in November 1935. Like the D.3 Gull Six of 1934, it was powered by the 200 hp DH Gipsy Six. A majority had the optional DH Gipsy Six Series II with the DH-PD30 VP airscrew. G-AFEA pictured here was a January 1938 production and its first owner was racing pilot Alex Henshaw. Restored at Fairoaks in 1947, it was sold abroad in July 1952.

The Vega Gull was a noteworthy aircraft in pre-war skies. Beryl Markham flew one, VP-KCC *The Messenger* from Abingdon to Nova Scotia in 21 hours on 4-5th September, 1936, the first solo east-to-west crossing by a woman. Two examples were entered for the Schlesinger Race from England to Johannesburg. G-AEKE flown by Scott and Guthrie was the only one to arrive at Rand Airport on October 1st, 1936, marking the culmination of a 52 hours 56 minutes 48 seconds flight from Portsmouth. Percival immediately set up a production line at larger premises at Luton. The Vega Gull was an immediate success with production running to 90, the last production aircraft making its maiden flight on July 27th, 1939. G-AEZJ, seen here, has had a fascinating history. Believed to be the sole remaining airworthy model, it dates from 1937 and was a participant in that years King's Cup Race finishing sixth. In March 1938 it was sold to the Netherlands becoming PH-ATH. Impounded by German invaders in May 1941 and impressed to Luftwaffe service as KE+CW, it was sold to neutral Sweden during 1942. Allocated the temporary German civil registration 'D-IXWD' for the ferry flight, the aircraft eventually became Swedish SE-ALA before returning to Britain in 1987 and taking up its original markings.

The Vega Gull was ideally suited to fast and economic transportation so unsurprisingly after the outbreak of war in September 1939, everybody who needed a communications aircraft sought out the Vega Gull with the result that the type was high on the requisition list. In Britain no fewer than 21 were impressed in 1939–40, one being G-AFIE, pictured here, which was first registered on July 25th, 1938. Its operator was Smith's Aircraft Instruments Ltd of Hatfield but it was destroyed in a German bombing raid on RAF Hendon on October 7th, 1940. By the war's end, the Vega Gull had been largely supplanted by the Proctor of which more than 1,100 were manufactured. Most Proctors, especially the later and heavier examples, lacked the nimble performance of the original Vegas, in particular as regards speed.

Eric Zander and Alfred Weyl formed a small business called Zander & Weyl Ltd of Dunstable and built the Dunstable Dart, a swept-wing parasol monoplane powered by a 27 hp Ava 4a.00 flat-four pusher engine and registered G-AELR. After Zander moved on to do his own thing, Weyl formed himself into Dart Aircraft Ltd and renamed the aircraft the Dart Pup. Underpowered in its original form, it was revised with a 36 hp Bristol Cherub III, horn-balanced rudder and an undercarriage that gave greater ground clearance. Sold to Alfred Edward Green in September 1937, he kept it at Tachbrook Aerodrome, Leamington. On August 31st, 1938, Green was attempting take-off from Wroxall Aerodrome near Kenilworth when it stalled and struck a boundary hedge sustaining terminal damage. It was claimed to have remained underpowered to the end. This picture shows it in its first form with the low undercarriage and Ava engine.

There's nothing more dangerous than a raw amateur who gets 'a good idea'. Usually somebody will suffer as a result. In the case of 40-year-old Richard Harold Taylor, pictured here, it would be him and the price to pay would be his life. Derbyshire-born in 1896, he was the son of a collier and in his early teens he had worked in the pits. At some time he came south to the privately-owned Hamsey Green Aerodrome near Warlingham in Surrey. Here he oversaw the construction of his brainchild – an all-metal tandem two-seater powered by one of the newly-built four cylinder inline Weir Pixie autogiro engines. The airframe was made of strips of metal but not quite Barnes Wallis's geodetic form which gave us the robust Wellington bomber. Taylor's wing, for example, had neither lift struts nor spars.

The often-meandering courses of his strips of metalwork ought to have alerted observers but one must assume there weren't any who might have had knowledge to raise the question of strength. While the fuselage was probably robust enough, the wings had absolutely nothing that might loosely be termed structural members. They supported the fabric covering but did little else.

Possibly somebody did say something because Taylor and his friend in plus-fours decided they could prove the strength by lifting the whole airframe off the ground using the wing. The absence of the engine, a person in the cockpit and some fuel probably reduced the dead weight by more than half. Factors of safety? Merely a confusion, old man. Merely a confusion…

It was January 7th, 1937. Apparently, Taylor had already made two or three flights in the finished Taylor Monoplane, G-AEPX – a total of 15 to 20 minutes. On his next attempt, shortly after this snapshot was taken, Taylor made a good take-off and turned into wind to land. At this point the port wing folded up and the machine plunged to earth. It was the cantilever wing which caused the crash. Subsequently, the Air Ministry's inspector of accidents found that 'the flight appeared to be in contravention of the regulations' adding that 'the pilot was not the holder of an A licence, and the flight was not authorized by the issue of a permit'. Interestingly, in this picture the rudder is appreciably larger than in other images.

In 1935 Mervyn Chadwick and Raymond Gordon had attempted to develop a business out of building Mignet's Flying Flea but after this was grounded they turned their attention to the low powered, low wing single seat monoplane market, then being served by the Belgian Tipsy S. The result was the Gordon Dove built by their business, Premier Aircraft Constructions Ltd formed in November 1936. A most attractive aircraft, it quickly proved to its makers that there wasn't a market for the open single-seater in Britain even at a selling price of £225. As a result, only three aircraft were built, G-AETU the prototype, G-AEZA and this one, G-AEZB. Just two weeks after being sold to John Keane Flower, it was damaged in a forced landing at Tilbury, Essex, on September 9th, 1937. Judging by the visible damage in this picture, it was quite repairable. *Picture by Harold Harvey*

Moss Brothers Aircraft Ltd was formed on January 1st, 1936, at 45 Ashfield Road, Chorley. The directors were William Henry Moss, Geoffrey P Moss, Brian E Moss, Ronald L Moss and Richard A S Moss and the aims of the company were 'the design, manufacture and repair of aircraft of all types'. The business produced just two sporting aircraft, the MA.1 and the MA.2. G-AEST, pictured here, was the former. Powered by a 95 hp Pobjoy Niagara III, it was an aerobatic open cockpit tandem two-seater first flown in 1937. *Aeroplane* magazine's test pilot Francis Delaforce Bradbrooke was greatly impressed with the performance. After the war it was turned into a single-seater for the 1950 King's Cup Race staged at Pendeford Airfield, Wolverhampton, on June 17th. Flown by owner-pilot William Moss, it stalled and spun in when making a steep turn over Newport, one of the turning points in the race. Mosscraft designer and managing director W H Moss was killed. This picture was taken at Birmingham in 1949.

Early in 1939, the company produced its second design, the Mosscraft MA.2, G-AFMS. Demonstrated at the Royal Aeronautical Society Garden Party staged at Sir Richard Fairey's private aerodrome at Heath Row, West London, in May 1939, this model differed from the earlier aircraft in having a 90 h.p Blackburn Cirrus Minor I inline engine and possessing a closed cabin. This aircraft was shipped to Canada in 1940 as CF-BUB and made a long cross-country flight from Vancouver, over the Rocky Mountains to Toronto and south to New York. Shipped back to the UK in 1947 and resuming its original identity, it took part in the King's Cup Race for 1950 and 1954. Now owned by the PFA's Swansea-based Fairwood Flying Group, on July 7th, 1958, it crashed ten miles south of Builth Wells, Mid-Wales. The pilot escaped, the aircraft did not – and that was the end of the Mosscraft.

Australian designer Geoffrey Neville Wikner, cousin of Edgar Percival, came to England in May 1934, his target being the making of the cheapest four-seat cabin aircraft. Using a Ford motor-car engine would keep costs down. In 1936 with two business partners, Victor 'Jack' Foster and furniture-maker James F Lusty he formed Foster, Wikner Aircraft Co Ltd. The firm began in Lusty's furniture factory in London's Bromley-by-Bow, and here they built a prototype named the Foster Wikner Wicko. The Ford engine gave the aircraft a streamlined nose but it was heavy and with it the aircraft was underpowered. The aircraft did not quality for a C of A without a proper aircraft engine so a Blackburn Cirrus Minor had to be fitted. Here Wikner poses with his first creation.

Having lost a major part of the aircraft's *raison d'etre*, the Wicko now competed on an open market. In 1937 the firm moved to Eastleigh Airport. The all-wood aircraft seemed set for success. Ten aircraft were made, the second, G-AEZZ, ready in time for the 1937 King's Cup Race. This had a 150 hp Cirrus Major engine but force-landed at Skegness and was unplaced. The rudder carried a small mass balance weight on a steel arm at its top.

G-AEZZ was far from unattractive as a light aircraft and, as with so many machines of this era, had war not intervened, it might have enjoyed a greater success. Later sold to Cardiff Aeroplane Club, it was impressed as ES943 on the outbreak of war but was scrapped in September 1943. One Wicko had an amazing escape. This one, G-AFJB, miraculously survived what on the face of it should have been a terminal event. It force-landed on Walney Island in poor visibility and fell over a cliff, dropping upside down into the sea below. Incredibly it was not smashed to pieces and still flies to this day.

The tenth and last Foster Wikner Wicko to be built was G-AGPE. It was intended to be the Wicko Warferry, a GM.1 in wartime regalia. In fact although it carried the markings HM497 at one time, it was stored during the war until found at Eastleigh by accident in 1946. Registered G-AGPE on April 4th that year, it was operated by notable former ATA pilot, Miss Philippa Bennett (1919-2007) who used it for charter work. It differed from other Wickos is that it had a socket for an external 'trolleyacc' starter battery just under the rear tear-drop window on the starboard side. The rudder was also larger with a small aerodynamic balance. It was withdrawn from use in July 1948 and scrapped at Eastleigh the following May.

Alfred Weyl's Dart Aircraft Ltd designed the single-seat Kitten in 1936. The prototype, G-AERP, had a 27 hp Ava 4a-00 flat four but was somewhat underpowered with this motor. It survived the war and, on November 23rd, 1952, crashed at Broxbourne killing its owner-pilot, Walter Scott Ogilvie. A second Kitten, slightly revised and fitted with a J.99 Aeronca JAP engine of 37 hp, was this one, G-AEXT. This had several accidents and rebuilds but still flies today. At the time this was built, Dart Aircraft made a complete kit of parts for a third aircraft which was stored, unassembled, on top of an internal office at Harrison's Garage at Loudwater outside High Wycombe. This was assembled in 1952 as G-AMJP but was lost in a crash at Hillington, King's Lynn, in June 1966. Pilot Geoffrey Bramhill survived.

Two former de Havilland Technical College students, the Hon Andrew William Henry Dalrymple and Alexander Reginald Ward shared a desire for a cheap to build and fly racing aircraft and so, in 1937, they designed and built the Chilton DW.1 single-seater. Power was provided by a 32 hp Carden-Ford conversion of a motor car engine modified with dual ignition and somewhat lightened. In April that year, the red and silver prototype, G-AESZ, was first flown at Witney in Oxfordshire. The all-wood low-wing monoplane had split trailing-edge flaps and all trailing edges –wing and tail surfaces – were made to a finely-crafted 'sharp' edge for streamlining. Five airframes were built; four completed including one DW.1a fitted with a French 45 hp Train 4T four-cylinder inverted inline engine.

Posed at Hungerford in 1938 is the second Chilton to be built, the blue and silver G-AFGH. All of the 1930s-made Chiltons survived the war but this suffered major damage in a forced landing at South Chalfont at the hands of Myles Bickerton, owner of Denham Aerodrome. This was on July 3rd, 1949, just days before the National Air Races in which the aircraft was entered. Speedy 'repairs' comprised borrowing the fuselage of G-AESZ and coupling on the wings of G-AFGH to the consternation of more than mere spotters. The hybrid, displaying two registrations, was completed just in time for Sqdn Ldr H R Bilborough to finish 13th in the Grosvenor Cup Race flying the hybrid Chilton at an average of 95.5 mph. Soon afterwards, proper repairs enabled 'ESZ to have its wings back, and 'FGH got a restored fuselage from the pre-war unfinished machine.

With its characteristically different shaped fin and rudder (the top is rounded instead of pointed), G-AFSV was the sole example of the DW.1a. It succeeded in breaking the 100 km international closed circuit record at 124.5 mph at Lympne Airfield on August 31st, 1947, flown by Ranald Porteous. The Chiltons were flown in a number of post-war air races for some years. The cleaned-up third aircraft, G-AFGI, was fitted with a cockpit canopy from an Olympia sailplane and given a 62 hp Walter Mikron engine. With these refinements it won the Daily Express Air Race at Shoreham Airport on September 22nd, 1951 at an average speed of 129 mph. Later it was refitted afresh with a 55 hp Lycoming flat four.

Besides the 'Hungerford Four' as they were once known, the incomplete fifth airframe, G-AFSW, was sacrificed for spares in the 1950s. Three new post-war Chiltons have been constructed by amateur builders under the auspices of the Light Aircraft Association following the successful preparation of a set of working drawings, partly original and partly newly-drawn from surviving components. The type remains as successful as ever. Comparisons are sometimes drawn between the Chilton and the Taylor-Watkinson Ding-Bat G-AFJA since both have similar parentage, were projected to fulfil similar goals and, initially, had the same engine. The reader must draw his/her own conclusions! The picture of G-AFSV was taken at Baginton on July 13th, 1957. The aircraft colour scheme was by then black and yellow.

The Hillson Praga was a licence-built Czechoslovakian aircraft – the Praga E114 Air Baby – dating from 1934. On August 15th, 1935, a demonstrator aircraft on a European tour, OK-PGB, visited Heston. As a result a Manchester woodworking company, F Hills & Sons Ltd of Trafford Park decided to build the aircraft in Britain. The engine was a Czech copy of the American Aeronca E.113C flat twin. Contemporary with this, Nicholas Comper of Comper Swift fame formed a consultancy with a friend, Francis R Walker, as Comper & Walker. Walker had been badly injured in the crash of one of Comper's Swifts, G-ACBY, at Moulton on July 8th, 1933, during the King's Cup Race. Now they imported a Praga, G-ADXL, for a sales tour of their own which attracted no business. Hills began production as the Hillson Praga and Jowett Cars started making the Praga B motor in Bradford, but could not get it certified. Hills then chose the 36 hp Aeronca JAP J.99, a British-made version of the Aeronca E.113C – so the engine went 'full circle'. Some 32 aircraft were built, 25 for the home market. Several survived the war but it was not really a successful aircraft. G-AEUT, seen here, was one of the last produced in 1938. The type is now extinct.

The Aeronca C-3 was built by the Aeronautical Corporation of America, Inc, at Lunken Airport, Cincinnati, Ohio. The decision was taken to manufacture this light two-seater in Britain and so the Aeronautical Corporation of Great Britain Ltd was founded in Peterborough. To begin with, Canadian agents the Murray Aeronautical Corporation supplied 16 American-built examples to Hanworth, the first two being demonstrated convincingly in high winds on September 19th, 1935. Using this aircraft with its low operating costs, London Air Park Flying Club at Hanworth advertised training to pilot's 'A' Licence for under £20. G-ADYR seen here is an example of that first batch. It was flown in the 1936 Folkestone Trophy Race by company test pilot Richard Grubb who won at the remarkable speed of 84.75 mph. The American-made Aeroncas are quickly distinguished by the lack of control mass-balances, the presence of corrugated metal ailerons, smooth, unbalanced profile of the fin and rudder, and the pressed aluminium rocker-box covers to the engine valve-gear.

After the encouraging reception given to the US-made Aeronca C-3, the Aeronautical Corporation of Great Britain Ltd began production at Peterborough of a British version called the Aeronca 100. It differed slightly from the original. For a start, chrome-molybdenum tube was not available in Britain so a different specification was used calling for a change of gauge in places. The metal ailerons were replaced by wooden ones and both ailerons and rudder were equipped with static mass-balances – an 'egg' of lead on the end of a steel tube. The rudder example was immediately obvious and defined the type. The pitot head was mounted above the centre-section pylon. The engine was an English-built version of the original – the J.99 flat-twin manufactured by J A Prestwich Ltd in London. Known for short as the 'JAP' engine, too many subsequent writers have mistaken this for an indication of oriental rather than occidental source. G-AEVT was the 10th of 21 examples built in Northamptonshire. Restored by Paul Simpson and the author, it was destroyed in a crash at Loughborough on July 11th, 1950.

G-AEVS was built as an Aeronca 100 but is seen here in flight with the American-made Aeronca E-113C engine distinguished by its pressed aluminium rocker-box covers – the JAP J.99 engine had a neat casting for this part with a cut-out in the lower edge to allow access to the bottom sparking-plug. Compare this picture with that of G-AEVT. This aircraft still flies. All US-made and British C-3s and 100s had only one door on the starboard side. This was not really convenient as your passenger (or, more usually, your luggage suitcase) was between you and the entrance-exit and had to be removed before you could get out.

The second aircraft to emerge from the Peterborough factory was G-AESP pictured here with a modified tail skid to incorporate a tail-wheel. Despite an initial wave of enthusiasm and a selling price of just £365, the Aeronca two-seater was not a great marketing success in Britain and ended up being sold off where possible by Aircraft Exchange & Mart Ltd at Hanworth. Some examples made extraordinary flights and one flew to Capetown. At the end of the war, sixteen were found and eleven flew again, including this one which lived at Elstree in the immediate post-war years in the care of A R 'Tiny' Pilgrim who somehow managed to fit his six-foot six-inch frame into the rather tight cockpit.

The Aeronautical Corporation of Great Britain Ltd combined under one roof a small business called Light Aircraft Ltd of Hanworth, engine-makers J A Prestwich Ltd, Lang Propellers Ltd, and Aircraft Accessories Ltd. A subsidiary was Aircraft Exchange & Mart Ltd at Hanworth. When formed on April 1st, 1936, it was funded to an astonishing £300,000. It moved in to the one-time factory of Frederick Sage Ltd, Great War aircraft makers. But things must have gone wrong very quickly for in a few months the business clocked up losses in excess of £72,000. After just 17 months of existence, Aeronca was bankrupt and on November 5th, 1937 it was would up. Almost immediately a new firm emerged called Peterborough Aircraft Ltd which promoted the Aeronca 300, G-AEVE.

The Aeronca 300 G-AEVE was not a 'new' design. Registered in July 1938, it was clearly a development of the 100. It was premiered at the Hatfield SBAC Show on June 29th in the name of Peterborough Aircraft Ltd. Wider than the conventional aircraft, it also had two cabin doors, one each side. The aircraft survived the war in poor storage and the wings went to the rebuild of G-AEVT whereupon it was found that G-AEVE must have been 12 inches wider than the normal 100: the aileron root end pulleys were each six inches further outboard than on 'EVT's original wings. At the time of its launch, the Aeronca 300 was restyled the Peterborough Ely 700 and two additional registrations allocated but not taken up. As late as July 1939, aircraft brokers W S Shackleton Ltd were offering brand new '100s' for £160.

Frederick Handley Page had a thing about bracing wires. Having used them extensively on the O/400 and its derivatives ending with the W8, W9 and W10, he concluded that they were fiddly and unnecessary. How much better to have a rigid steel tube! Assembly and rigging time was far quicker that way, he reckoned. And so when he specified the HP.42 for Imperial Airways Ltd, there wasn't a bracing wire in sight! When prototype G-AAGX took off on its maiden flight at Radlett in November 1930, all one saw was a splendid array of bracing struts like a railway bridge. In tests, however, certain twisting loads to the top wing overhang proved more than estimated and the giant airliner landed with the outermost bay diagonal buckled. The answer was to replace it with a pair of diagonal bracing wires… This picture was taken half an hour before that diagonal nearest the camera bent in the middle. On another topic, notice how the airfield boundary trees have all been topped.

The de Havilland DH.91 Albatross was an aircraft that represented just about everything that was good, bad and doubtful in an airliner design. It endured a curious history but ultimately gave indirect inspiration to one of the most successful and respected airliners of all times. Like so many leaps in design faith, though, there are times when it does not pay to be first. Arthur Ernest Hagg designed the DH.91 in 1936 to an Air Ministry specification that called for a pair of transatlantic mailplanes. The prototype, E.2/G-AEVV, took to the air for the first time on May 20th, 1937 at the hands of company test pilot Robert John Waight. Other than its two curiously braced fins and rudders that looked like an afterthought, it bore no resemblance to anything that had previously emerged from the DH works.

Aerodynamically refined, the range was an astonishing 3,000 miles at a cruising speed in excess of 200 mph. Everyone agreed that it was an outstanding performer beside being one of the most beautiful aircraft ever built. But the second prototype, E.5/G-AEVW *Franklin*, revealed a design oversight. On August 27th, 1938, it was undergoing flight trials at maximum weight with a 3,000 lb overload and, on the third landing, the plywood monocoque fuselage suddenly broke completely in half. There was a large oval cut-out for a door on each side of the sleek body exactly where it broke! The Albatross lay on Hatfield's finely-mown grass in two very distinct pieces. It was quickly gathered up and a new fuselage, now made with doors distanced on each side, fitted. Lesson One.

The DH.91 had four new and untried engines – 525 hp Gipsy Twelve inverted V-type – buried in the wings and aspirated through leading-edge airways. DH constant-speed propellers were fitted. The combination was an outstanding success and the mail version, of which there were two, had a maximum speed of 222 mph while the passenger variant, five in all, could top 225 mph with a cruising speed of 210 mph and an initial rate of climb of 710 ft/min. It had an inwards-retracting undercarriage with, of course, single wheels of large diameter. Another improvement was to replace the antiquated vertical tail surfaces with modern end plate style.

Deliveries to Imperial Airways began in October 1938. Here G-AFDI *Frobisher* is readied for loading at Croydon. By a prophetic coincidence in the skies above it there flies a DC-2, an all-metal aircraft that could be parked out in the open all night in any weather. The DH.91 was made entirely of wood and had to be hangared at night. The DC-2 came to pieces quite easily for maintenance and repair. The Albatross had a finely-made but rather inconvenient one-piece wing. In other words, damage to one wing-tip meant the entire 105 foot span wing had to be shipped off for repairs. Oh dear! Lesson Two…

The DH.91 mailplane, G-AEVV *Faraday*, displays its revised and modern-looking vertical tail surfaces in the fine shot of G-AEVV. These were known as the 'F' Class fleet for they all had names that began with that letter. The passenger version carried 22 passengers and four crew. In those final months up to the outbreak of war, the aircraft settled down to operate a fast and profitable scheduled service from Croydon to Paris, Brussels and Zurich not to mention a Christmas mail flight to Cairo. On January 10th, 1939, G-AFDJ *Falcon* landed at Brussels 48 minutes after leaving Croydon. Ah! Things were fine! But war loomed.

Once war was declared, the DH.91s were seconded to other duties. The two mailplanes were impressed as AX903 and AX904, while the others provided a restricted and wartime priority airline service. Here we see G-AEVW as AX904 in camouflage livery. None was to enjoy a rich or long life for it was found that even minor damage called for major dismantling. And the test scenario happened when, far from home, one did indeed damage a wing-tip. Uneconomical to dismantle and send the whole wing back to Hatfield, the aircraft was scrapped. This was the story of them all ultimately. Lesson three… But in better times when Lockheed chose to design an all-American airliner, it was to the Albatross that the company looked for its lines. And so the 1951 skies displayed the fine lines of the last good-looking piston-engined airliner. I am sure many of us have flown in a Constellation since those days!

Despite what one might term the 'mechanical prejudice' against American aircraft, there were certain types of US aeroplanes that appealed to aspects of the British market. In the 1930s one of these was the Stinson Reliant. In keeping with aircraft from this part of the world, they were frequently differentiated by a mixture of letters and numerals rather than names and the SR series was a good example. There were many varieties and G-AEVY was an SR-9D Reliant. First registered here on May 18th, 1937, it was impressed as W7984 in February 1940 but seems to have been 'cancelled' less than three weeks later. It is pictured here at Heston shortly after its arrival from America.

Designer Leslie Baynes had an idea for a novel type of twin engined light aircraft. He took out a patent in December 1933 for a cantilever-winged aeroplane with a one-piece wing that was pivoted at the centre section so the whole mainplane could be rotated through 90 degrees to lie parallel and on top of the fuselage for low-space storage. Power came from two sideways-mounted Carden-Ford modified Ford car engines as developed by Sir John Carden. In December 1935, Carden lost his life in an air crash but Baynes went on to form Carden-Baynes Aircraft Ltd in his memory the following April. The Bee was registered G-AEWC and first flew at Heston on 3rd April 1937, in the hands of Hubert Broad. It suffered from engine cooling problems, was sluggish in handling both in the air and on the ground while its narrow-track wheels did nothing to aid cross-wind taxiing let alone landings. Possible corrections were overtaken by financial problems, and bankruptcy in June 1937 put the brakes on future development. Sale of rights to the design to newly-formed Scottish Aircraft Construction Co Ltd went nowhere and the Bee was broken up at Heston in the summer of 1935.

The Parnall Type 382 was a two-seat ab initio trainer to Air Ministry Spec T.1/37. Designed by Basil Henderson it was based on the Heck 2C, it was larger and heavier than the Miles Magister which it loosely resembled. The engine was a 200 hp Gipsy Six and it had outer wing panels, tail unit and a fixed undercarriage similar to the earlier Heck. The first primary trainer to have interconnected slots and flaps, the camber-changing flaps could be lowered to 45 degrees while the outer sections were used as ailerons. Test flown at Yate by company test pilot James A Crosby Warren, the Type 382 was dived at 265 mph. The machine could be flown from either cockpit without change of ballast and the front cockpit emulated controls for a larger aircraft including landing gear retraction system. The sole example flew as J.1 but was later allocated G-AFKF. Impressed as R9138, it never attracted production status and was scrapped during the war.

The Hornet Moth was another difficult aircraft when launched at Hatfield. It went through several incarnations before emerging as the fine, reliable and safe two-seater that still flies today. The DH.87 first flew on May 9th, 1934 and Geoffrey de Havilland piloted it in the subsequent King's Cup Race. Teething problems saw the original elliptical shaped wing-tips replaced by slender tapered ones. The designation became DH.87A. After 164 examples, production suddenly changed to wings with only the slightest of taper and squared-off tips. Now called the DH.87B, owners were invited to exchange their old tapered wings for new ones. Huge popularity the world over proved Hatfield now had it right. During the war the DH.87B was a popular liaison aircraft and many were called up. Not surprisingly a number still fly. Impressed as W5777, G-AEWY of March 1937, was restored but crashed at Barton in April, 1964.

A Dutch oddity was the single-seat pusher Schelde Scheldemusch, designed by Theodor Slot (1855-1949) as an ultra-safe unstallable replacement for Mignet's Flying Flea. The engine was a 40 hp Praga B2. An aircraft was brought to demonstrate before the press at Gravesend on March 3rd, 1937. Demonstration pilot was Robert Galloway Doig (1914-1966) who had also been interested in Fleas and was hoping to have made money out of a replacement. Sadly his attempt to show off the safety of the Scheldt Sparrow PH-AMA appeared to centre on bad flying and the inevitable crash, while not fatal, ended his hopes. Surprisingly a further example, PH-AMG, was brought to the UK and was briefly considered by the RAF. In 1945 it was offered for sale at £235. No sale was forthcoming although the airframe was said to have survived until 1960.

Most of my pictures are of civilian aircraft but I could not resist this one of an Avro Anson I, K6174, giving an impression of an alligator lurking in the shallows of Dovercourt Bay, Harwich in Essex (not Kent as suggested elsewhere), on the afternoon of December 1st, 1938. In heavy rain and poor visibility the trainee pilot put down in the sea and the wooden-winged Avro floated well enough to allow local boatmen to get alongside. As it was the French who gave us the language of aviation, here we have a clear-cut case of amerrisage rather than atterrisage!

Now largely forgotten is this, one of the clever, trend-setting light aircraft of the pre-war days. Morris B Arpin (1895-1975) had been a draughtsman at Faireys but after working on the Swordfish he left to start his own aircraft business at West Drayton, Middlesex. His real goal, though, was a safe, low-cost trainer aircraft that would incorporate not just the newly-invented tricycle format, but have the castoring wheels designed by Owen F Maclaren. The first design, unbuilt, had two tandem seats, a single tail boom and a 1,000cc JAP engine. Significantly, Arpin's AR-1 design, when it appeared, was similar in appearance to the US Stearman-Hammond 'Y' which it pre-dated by half a decade.

Arpin's target was an easy-to-fly robust wooden aircraft which would sell to the man-in-the-street for £300. The AR-1 was the outcome. A pod fuselage seating two in tandem was carried on a cantilever wing to which were affixed a pair of diamond cross section booms that carried the twin fin-and-rudder tail assembly. Power came from a 68 hp British Salmson AD.9R radial arranged as a pusher. The first flight of G-AFGB was made by George Wynne-Eyton on May 7th, 1938, at Hanworth. It was the first British aircraft to be designed to take a tricycle landing gear and Maclaren's design allowed all three wheels to be turned parallel to each other but not necessarily to the aircraft, so that cross wind landings could be made with the aircraft pointing into wind. The front wheel could be left to castor or could be steered by the pilot.

Engine cooling troubles were an early problem solved in part by re-engining the aircraft with a 90 hp Cirrus Minor I. Now with its bugs sorted, and with fine reviews from evaluation pilots who admired the excellent view over the nose, Arpin was ready for production but war intervened. He tried to get the military interested but it required costly development to attain that type of usage. Arpin's little company didn't have the money. The Arpin was stored during the war but by 1946 it was deemed no longer viable and was sold for scrap. A sad end to a worthwhile effort. Morris Arpin went on to design and build the first 'air bridge' passenger walkways for use at airports.

Eric T Watkinson and Cyril W Taylor were students at the de Havilland Technical College at Hatfield. Taylor was 21 years old in 1936 when he began his design from a single seat ultra-light monoplane fitted with a 30 hp Carden-Ford water-cooled engine. His goal was to produce sets of plans for sale. The two men formed a partnership based at Teddington, Middlesex and, inspired by the success of the Chilton monoplane, also the work of DH technical college students, they built their aircraft and called it the Ding-Bat. It was registered G-AFJA. The bluff blue and white ultra-light first flew at Heston on August 2nd, 1938, at the hands of Ranald Porteous who had also flown the slightly smaller, lighter and faster but same-engined Chilton. Stored during the war, it was sold for £50 to the Experimental Group of the Ultra Light Aircraft Association in May, 1948, but restoration took 11 years. Now painted bright yellow with blue wings, a bad crash in 1975 led to a further rebuild.

Cecil Hugh Latimer-Needham designed the Luton LA.2, 3 and 4 Minor single seaters in the late 1930s in response to the Flying Flea hiatus. Spurred on by the success of that venture he made a tandem two seater called the LA.5 Major powered by a 62 hp Walter Mikron II in-line inverted four-cylinder air-cooled engine. Only one was ever built and G-AFMU is seen here at Denham on the occasion of its maiden flight by Sqdn Ldr Edward Lucas Mole. Demonstrated at Heathrow on the occasion of the Royal Aeronautical Society Garden Party on May 14th, 1939, it attracted much favourable attention. War put a stop on a six-strong production batch and the prototype aircraft was destroyed in a factory fire in 1943. After the war, Phoenix Aircraft revised the aircraft as the LA.6 Major

Pictured soon after completion, the folding-winged Luton Major had horizontally-split Piper Cub-style cockpit doors where half hinged downwards and the other upwards to clip into the underside of the wing. During the war it was housed with the Luton Minor and the part-finished airframes of six other aircraft at the Phoenix Garage, Tatling End, Gerrards Cross, which burned to the ground during the machining of magnesium castings during the war years. The plant was rebuilt but Luton Aircraft did not survive the war.

Percival Nesbitt Willoughby, pictured at the left with his prototype, was a man with a vision – one of a 100 foot-plus span flying-wing airliner having three engines and accommodating 18 (later 36) passengers in a cabin contained within the depth of each wing. This goal was announced in February of 1939. It was to be the climax of a London-based company named the Willoughby Delta Co which had been formed on October 8th, 1931, with £1,500 capital. Such an unusual design called for much preparatory wind tunnel work and this was carried out at the National Physical Laboratory, the City & Guilds, Farnborough, and Queen Mary College, London. Valuable pressure distribution measurements were made in the United States at New York University's Guggenheim Institute. The results were encouraging, producing curves of lift coefficient versus angle of incidence that increased linearly in the normal way and then flattened without the usual decrease in lift associated with the stall. It appeared that, at high speed and low angles the forward part of the wing provided most of the lift, but as the stall approached the rear part contributed more. Willoughby also studied the work of American Vincent Burnelli and his Flying Wing airliners.

Willoughby's small twin-engined proof-of-concept aircraft called the Willoughby Delta 8 displays its radical profile. Registered G-AFPX, this was first flown by Archibald Norman Kingwill who went on to demonstrate the twin 125 hp Menasco Pirate C.4-powered prototype at the RAeS Garden Party at Heathrow on May 14th, 1939. Right from the start the small 34 ft 6-inch span aircraft flew well and proved to be virtually unstallable. Work went on with the larger Delta 9 seen as a realistic approximation to a true flying wing, with its advantage of a well-distributed load because of the absence of parts like a fuselage which did not contribute to lift.

The four-cylinder air-cooled inline engines driving two-bladed propellers were mounted against the underside of the wing in steel cradles, at the points where the wing thickness increased. There was a wooden fairing behind, through which extended to the front spar and also mounted the fixed main undercarriage legs which were faired and spatted. The tailplane joined the rearmost inner edges of the side wings, carrying the tailwheel at its centre, and a broad elevator. On July 10th, 1939, having taken off from Minster Lovell Aerodrome (later Witney) in Oxfordshire during one of many hitherto successful test-flights, an elevator trim-tab malfunctioned due to a cable jumping a fairlead and pulley. The sudden elevator  deflection caused the Delta 8 to crash at Caulcott near Bicester. The pilot, 24-year-old Hugh Nichol Olley, chief instructor of the Witney & Oxford Aero Club, was killed along with his passenger, 36-year-old Percival Willoughby. With the death of the designer and the imminence of war, the project faded.

The Tipsy Trainer was the British-built development of Ernest Oscar Tips' Tipsy B series of aircraft, these in turn developed from the single-seater Tipsy S. Built at Slough, the Trainer underwent several crucial developments from its Belgian original. Prone to dropping a wing in a stall, sometimes unpredictably sharply, the fourth aircraft to emanate from the factory had a strengthened wing incorporating washout to delay tip-stall as well as camber-changing flaps to the parallel centre section. To satisfy UK airworthiness flutter concerns, all control surfaces were mass-balanced. At the same time, the original swept forward separate elevators were united into one straight-hinged assembly. From the 6th aircraft forwards, fixed letter-box wing slots became standard features of the wings. During the Certificate of Airworthiness tests at Martlesham Heath in August 1938, there were concerns about rudder authority, so 18% was added to the rudder area. At that point, the name was changed from Tipsy B to Tipsy Trainer. Meanwhile the 9th aircraft was approved at an increased all up-weight of 1,200 lb and from then on the name was revised to Tipsy Trainer 1 with a selling price of £550. In all, Tipsy Light Aircraft, with its sales office at Hanworth, made 18 aircraft, all with open cockpits. The last three were completed after the war, the final example flying in April 1948. Registered on August 5th, 1939, just weeks before the outbreak of war, G-AFWT was the 13th Tipsy Trainer to be built and so did not really feel the skies until after the conflict was over. Still flying today, it is captured in this fine picture taken at Old Warden on July 2nd, 2006, by Air-Britain's Brian Bickers.

Shanklin on the Isle of Wight has the distinction of being associated with not just one but three aerodromes. The first was Apse Heath or Apse Manor where Charles Coombes, a Shanklin motor-coach proprietor, based his Simmonds Spartan G-AAHA in June 1929. In May 1930 a company called Inland*[sic]* Flying Services rented land at Apse Manor Farm from a Mr and Mrs Fisk. Here, in 1932, a Boulton & Paul hangar was erected for the renamed Portsmouth, Southsea & Isle of Wight Aviation which operated an air taxi service from Portsmouth to Shanklin. It was joined by a bright red Spartan Three-seater G-ABAZ *Island Queen*, G-AAHA having been sold to South Africa as ZS-ADC in March of 1932. Early in 1934, Shanklin Flying Services was sold to a Mr and Mrs Ernest Byrne together with the G-ABAZ. During this time the airfield was relocated to larger fields just to the north and renamed Shanklin Aerodrome. The Byrnes then bought Lea Farm, about one mile further north of Apse and made that into an aerodrome in time for the 1935 season. In February 1935 they formed Sandown & Shanklin Flying Services Ltd, a private company which absorbed Shanklin Flying Services. Shortly before the war this was renamed Sandown Airport, *aka* Isle of Wight Airport. A long introduction to a snapshot of G-ABAZ at the old Apse Heath landing ground. I had several joy-rides in this fine veteran which was withdrawn from use on June 26th, 1939.

The de Havilland DH.94 Moth Minor was a sort of 'gentleman's Miles Magister' – a tandem two-seater low-winger that was fun to fly. With a 90 hp Gipsy Minor inverted inline four-cylinder engine up front, the Minor was a delight to fly. This one, G-AFRY, has an interesting history. More than 100 Moth Minors had been made at Hatfield by the time war started, whereupon all the partially-built airframes were shipped out to Australia where the indigenous de Havilland business could complete them. Of the ones made at Hatfield, nine were built as cabin aircraft, one being this example completed in July, 1939. During the war it flew as X5123 and then was restored by W A Rollason Ltd at Croydon in 1946. The opportunity was taken to convert it back to an open two-seater in which condition it flew at Cowes before going to Perth where it was withdrawn from use on December 10th, 1951. In this view, the port wing is folded back, the tip being visible behind the rudder.

Mention the pre-war American Piper Cub and one instantly thinks of the familiar and docile tandem two-seater J-2 where the pilot sits behind his passenger and wipes his feet on the trousers of the poor fellow in front of him. But there was another – the side-by-side two-seat J-4A Cub Coupé of which 24 were registered in Britain between its introduction in 1938 and the outbreak of war. G-AFSZ was imported, as were all of the tubular-steel, fabric-covered high-wingers, by A J Walter at Hanworth. It went to the Wiltshire School of Flying

but on the outbreak of war it was impressed as BT440. On January 29th, 1946, it resumed its civil career. On May 30th, 1962, it took off from the private airstrip of pilot-owner Edward Robert Barker at Cranleigh, Surrey, to fly the short distance to Fairoaks. A very heavy landing at the popular field north of Woking broke its back. Tentative plans to rebuild came to nought and the aircraft was finally scratched from the civil register on July 10th, 1962. My picture here was taken on May 2nd, 1959.

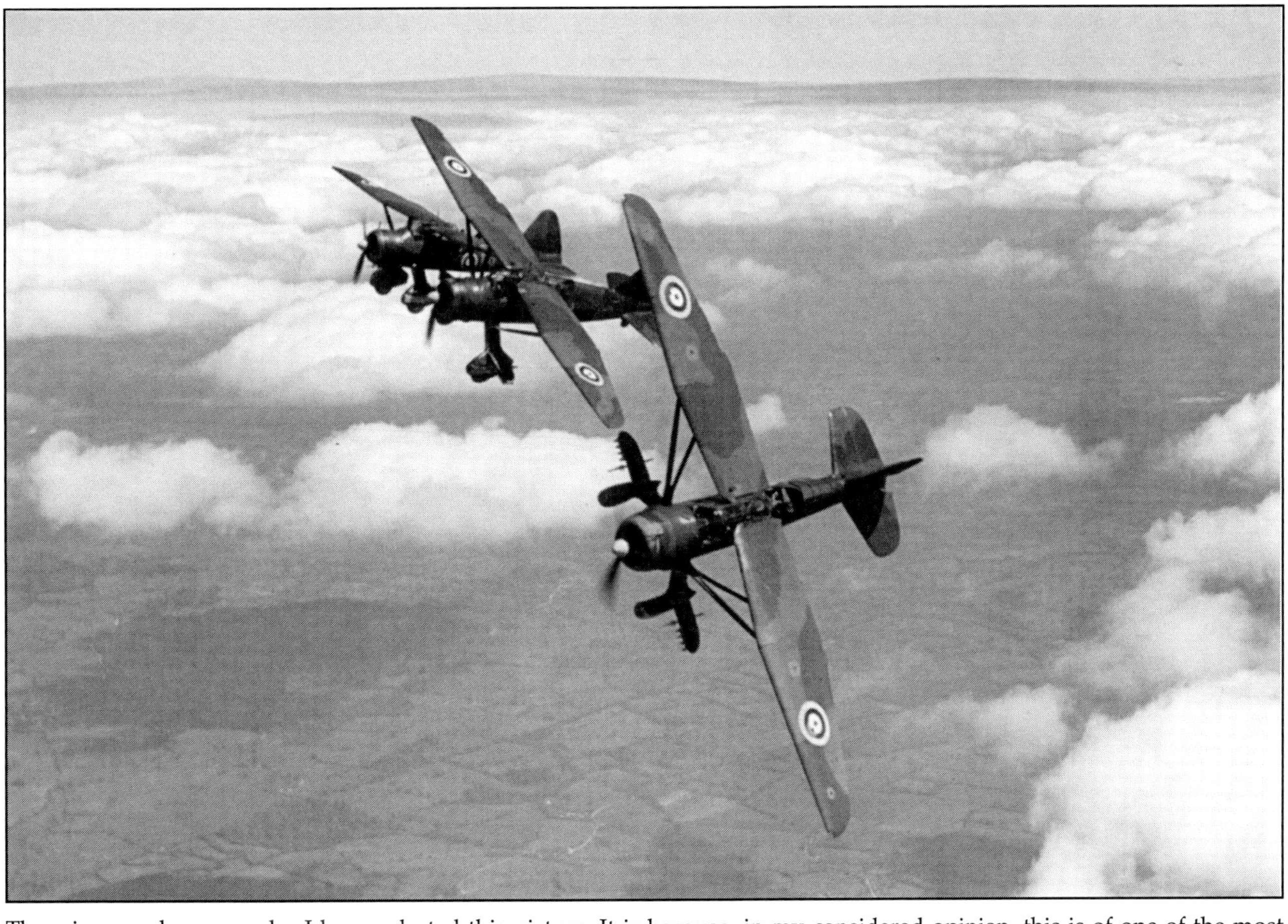

There is a good reason why I have selected this picture. It is because, in my considered opinion, this is of one of the most important pioneering STOL aircraft ever built. The Westland Lysander was actually created in response to a 1934 Air Ministry Specification which called simple for an army co-operation aircraft. Designer Arthur Davenport working with William Edward Willoughby Petter created an aircraft with exceptional short-field performance which made possible incredible RAF missions during the war to position and retrieve our wartime agents and spies often at night, especially operating in France where there was invaluable help from the French Resistance. Aerodynamically advanced, the Lysander wing was equipped with automatic slats and slotted flaps which, together with a variable-incidence tailplane, gave the aircraft a stalling speed of just 65 mph. These devices, together with numerous refinements, gave the production machine a STOL performance that was hitherto undreamed of except in experimental aircraft. The 'steps' on the wheel spats were bomb-racks, dispensed with in service. Besides an excellent pilot cockpit view, the Lysander was a ground-breaker, the next step being the post-war Prestwick Pioneer.

The Hawker Tomtit was created by designer Sydney Camm as a training biplane as a long-overdue replacement for the Avro 504K. Powered by a 150 hp Armstrong Siddeley Mongoose five-cylinder radial, the Tomtit was a single-bay biplane with a tubular steel frame fuselage and duralumin dumbbell-section wing spars, the whole aircraft fabric covered. Handley Page type automatic slots were fitted to the upper wings. The prototype first flew at the hands of George Bulman in November 1928. Some 35 Tomtits were built, five being civil. Of these five, the survivor is G-AFTA which was restored by its makers in 1949. Painted blue and white, it was the star performer at many a post-war air-show.

In 1935, nine ex-RAF Hawker Tomtits joined the original five on the civil register. After the war, two or three survived. One of these, G-AFVV was lost soon after the war and by 1947 there was just G-AFTA. This was always a popular performer because it had the lines of the top Hawker fighters of the 1930s and was fully aerobatic. In 1960 it was donated to the Shuttleworth Collection at Old Warden where it still performs. The one main difference is that today it is finished in Royal Air Force colours – all-silver finish complete with roundels plus the authentic marks K1786.

A fine example of a 'thirties Austrian aircraft was the Hirtenberg HS9A. In July, 1937, John Henry Davis of South London decided to buy one. He placed his order with the Hirtenberger Patronen Zündhutchen und Metallwarenfabrik AG situated in the small town of Hirtenberg near Baden bei Wien in Lower Austria, not far from the Vienna Woods. Built as OE-DJH, when it flew to England in July 1939, it bore the registration D-EDJH and carried a Nazi *Hakenkreuz* on its vertical tail surfaces. Less than two months later the war started and all civilian flying was prohibited. On November 22nd, 1939, the HS9A was accorded both a British C of A and the registration G-AGAK. It then went straight into store at Filton until transported to Gatwick for overhaul in 1946. It had several private owners thereafter until finally it ended up with Charles Henry 'Jack' Cosmelli and John Ernest Coxon. The Hirtenberg undertook a lot of flying from its base at either Denham or Elstree. On February 15th, 1958, Cosmelli set off from Denham to Bembridge with a friend. Butser Hill near Petersfield was topped by low cloud; Cosmelli flew into mist which had a very hard centre. G-AGAK was wrecked beyond repair and the two occupants escaped with minor injuries.

The story of the General Aircraft GAL.42 Cygnet is somewhat involved. It started life as a 1936 design by Carl R Chronander and James I Waddington who, along with J A Heron as chief engineer, had formed C W Aircraft at Hanworth to manufacture their aircraft in quantity. The unique feature of their design was that it was for an all-metal lightplane with metal skinning to both wings and fuselage. The prototype featured in that famous RAeS Garden Party at Heathrow in May, 1937, but CW Aircraft was about to suffer a problem that was common to so many companies. Underfunded and financially overstretched, it could not survive. Fortunately, the design was taken on by General Aircraft Ltd, a fellow Hanworth company. General Aircraft made some significant changes, not the least being the fitting of a tricycle undercarriage and, later, replacing the single fin and rudder with a twin tail. This gave us the Cygnet II as pictured here in G-AGBN. Much of these changes was the work of GAL designer and pilot David Hollis Williams (1900-1974). Including the prototype, nine aircraft were built and this is the only survivor. While the Cygnet was nice to fly with well-harmonised controls, it was extremely noisy in the enclosed cockpit because there was no insulation or other form of sound-proofing.

The Fane F1/40 Air Observation Post, G-AGDJ, was a particularly interesting design which was offered to the Air Ministry for mixed duties but was ultimately rejected and scrapped. Gerard William Reginald Fane was born in 1898 and educated at Charterhouse. He served in the RNAS during the First World War having lied about his age. He distinguished himself by his involvement in the successfull shooting down of Zeppelin L21 from his BE.2C in 1916, an act that earned him the DSC. In the 'thirties he owned Comper Swift G-AAZF and became involved with Nicholas Comper, ultimately becoming closely involved with him to the point where he formed Comper Fane Aircraft Ltd, a business registered on August 9th, 1939 – six weeks after Comper had been killed in a drunken prank. The new business was to take over the designs rights to the Comper Fly and Scamp, the projects in hand when their designer lost his life.

The Mikron-powered Comper Fly, under construction at Norbury and later finished off at Brooklands when war broke out, marked Comper's attempt to rebuild his former aircraft business which was taken over and finished off by the formation of Heston Aircraft Ltd in June 1934. The new company got rid of all the Comper directors in a slate-cleaning operation. And so the Fly was never completed but Fane took its shape to design his F1/40 pictured here. Fane ultimately changed the name of the new company to Fane Aircraft Ltd, this change taking effect on April 16th, 1940. This shift effectively eradicated all associations with Nicholas Comper. The Fane company now produced a rugged side-by-side two-seat pusher. Gone was Comper's elegant twin-boom wooden fuselage, this replaced by a narrow tapered welded tubular-steel box mounting a single tail with fixed fin and aerodynamically balanced rudder also with static mass-balance.

Fane's F1/40 was officially designed to Air Ministry specification F.1/40 for an airborne observation post. It was developed from a Comper design called the Scamp which had been projected as a two-seater but then altered to a single seater which he had named the Fly. Fane had taken the Scamp design and reworked it as his F.1 powered by an 80 hp Continental A-80 air-cooled flat-four engine. It is believed that the choosing of an American engine rather than a British-made one, especially in time of war, contributed to the aircraft's subsequent rejection by the 'powers that be'. On completion, it was taken on charge at Heston, now operating as a RAF acceptance unit. Here the Fane was given the markings T1788 and it was flown and evaluated by the Air Ministry at Heston in March 1941.

The Fane F1/40 had a length of 23 feet 5 inches and a wing-span of 37 feet. The maximum take-off weight was 1,500 lbs. As far as the Air Ministry Specification was concerned, it was in competition with the General Aircraft GAL.47 but in the end neither was selected for service use. On September 11th, 1941, the aircraft was registered G-AGDJ. An Authorisation to Fly was issued the following week to its constructors, but the aircraft appears to have undertaken little flying and it was scrapped during the war years. Gerard Fane later formed a company called Fane Engineering Designs Ltd at West Molesey, but he seems never again to have made an aircraft. He died in 1979.

The Monospar series of aircraft marked something of a triumph for Helmuth J Stieger and his novel method of wing-construction. As related in the book *The Monospar* (published by Stenlake, 2013), his lightweight yet strong metal design revolutionised the manner in which certain types of aircraft were built in the mid-'thirties. Here is a fine shot of a particularly interesting Monospar ST-25 Universal. The last to be registered in Britain, G-AGBN had been one of five special freighter aircraft originally made for Eastern Canada Air Lines, Ltd. These all had a large starboard loading hatch and had been handed over to their new owners by Lady Shelmerdine, wife of the then Director-General of Civil Aviation, at a naming ceremony held at Hanworth on September 28th, 1936. This one had been CF-BAH *City of Halifax*. Now returned to its makers on the outbreak of war, CF-BAH was registered here in November 1941 and flew as a communications aircraft throughout the war. Note the red, white and blue stripes painted on the fins and beneath the registration letters – the wartime requirements for civil aircraft that were allowed to operate on official business – together with camouflage paint scheme and an all-over bright yellow underside. After the war it became the private runabout of Fairey test pilot Cyril Geoffrey Marmaduke Alington at Gatwick but was scrapped in January 1947.

During the early part of the war, the Air Ministry acquired two Monospar ST-25 Universal aircraft. These were constructors' number 74 (L4671) pictured here, and constructors' number 76 (L4672). These were evaluated for Service duty as communications aircraft but in the end they were rejected on the grounds that they were two lightly-constructed and low-powered – the very reasons why they were built, for users found the advantage in light construction was the bonus of good performance on low power. However, there was little doubt that the Air Ministry would have preferred more weight and a lot more power using much more fuel to earn a tick on its requirements balance-sheet. *Picture by Mark Amor.*

Not one to cross paths with, this looks like a straight forward Rapide but in fact it is a rare example with a pretty vicious sting. The DH.89M was a military variant made by the Hatfield manufacturer. Initially allocated the markings K4772, it was an unsuccessful contender for the contract that ultimately went to the much larger Anson. The DH.89M went on to see service in Spain and Lithuania. This example was first registered to de Havilland on December 2nd, 1935, and allocated the registration G-ADYM. Two months later, on February 7th 1936 the registration was cancelled on its sale abroad. In fact it went off to fight in the Spanish Civil War joining the Spanish Air Force as 22-3. Note the additional cabin window and the dorsal fin. Its armament comprised one Vickers Mk.V machine gun on the starboard side of the nose (visible in this picture), and a Lewis Mk.III on top of the rear fuselage, It could also carry two 100 lb bombs or four at 20 lb. The aircraft was captured by Nationalists at Zaragoza on July 18th, 1937, and its crew of three shot. The aircraft now assumed a new identity as 40-5. That August 27th, this aircraft and two others (40-1 and 40-4) were involved in a bombing raid on the Sierra de Madrid when they were intercepted and mistaken for enemy aircraft by three Heinkel He-51s. DH.89M 40-5 was shot down over Turégano near Segovia and the entire crew killed – a tragic case of 'death by friendly fire'.

The name British European Airways conjours up memories of the last major airline to operate real aeroplanes like DH.89A Dragon Rapides. This one was built as a DH.89B Dominie for the RAF and its wartime identity was NR681. On February 2nd, 1945, it became G-AGLP and was worked hard from Northolt and Croydon until being withdrawn from use at the latter airfield in September of 1950. The Dragon Rapide was a fun aeroplane to fly, partly because it was such a small and narrow cockpit that you felt certain it had to be a smaller aeroplane! Then there was the disconcerting moment when, on take-off, the tail came up. You, in the nose, went down quite appreciably: it took a bit of getting used to.

The Beneš-Mráz Be-501 Bibi, G-AGSR, was a really fine aeroplane. With an all-up weight of only 1,144 lbs, this all-wood side-by-side two-seater was well-designed and beautifully built. The cabin was finished in deep crimson complete with sliding curtains in the roof quarter-lights. The engine was the 62 hp Walter Mikron inverted inline. Designed by Pavel Beneš and Jaroslav Mráz and first flown in 1936, the Be-501 was one of a small sequence of similar sporting and touring aircraft to emanate from this tiny Czechoslovakian workshop at Chocen. It is believed that fewer than a dozen were built and this one was originally OK-BET, constructors' number 2 and imported into Britain in 1938. Stored during the war it was acquired by H Clive-Smith who shared it with the Experimental Group of the 1946-founded Ultra Light Aircraft Association. Lovingly maintained but seldom flown, the aircraft had superbly-balanced controls and, while a little underpowered, was a delight to fly. Eventually, when the Experimental Group moved to Redhill, it was sold to M C Chorlton who took it to White Waltham for C of A renewal. On October 25th, 1951, after servicing it was flown by owner-pilot racing-car driver/designer, Bugatti Club member and film-director 37-year-old Michael C Chorlton (1913-1951) with 24-year-old Tom Manley as passenger. A few minutes after take-off it crashed close to the church of St John the Baptist in nearby Shottesbrooke Park. Both men were killed. The aileron cables were found to be crossed.

An aircraft which was much admired in 1947 but was prevented from enjoying well-deserved success was the twin-engined six-seater Portsmouth Aerocar, an in-house project by Portsmouth Aviation Ltd. The Aerocar was a star turn at the SBAC air shows of 1948 and 1949 at Radlett and it seemed on course for a good future. It was intended to be an aircraft that could be used for a variety of tasks. The Aerocar concept was conceived, developed and promoted by Lionel Balfour with much of the design being the responsibility of fellow director Flt Lt Francis Luxmoore. An unusual feature was that the fuselage had integral fixed skids so that in the event of a hydraulic failure, a safe wheels-up landing could be made. The prototype, originally known as the Aerocar Major, G-AGTG, and powered by two 155 hp Cirrus Major engines, was first flown from Portsmouth Airport in the late afternoon of June 18th, 1947. The pilot was Luxmoore himself in the absence of company test pilot Alan Jones.

Incorporating a number of other novel features, the Aerocar had a sound-proofed gondola fuselage, retractable tricycle undercarriage and variable pitch propellers. A great deal of interest was shown at the SBAC events and the makers quickly garnered a goodly-sized order-book. Development of the Aerocar was dependent on a licence manufacturing tie-up with India and negotiations had reached an encouragingly advanced state when the uncertainty arising from the partition of India in 1947 put a halt to them. Portsmouth Aviation was both too small and underfunded to continue alone. Talks with Auster Aircraft Ltd at Rearsby and Portsmouth Airport's Airspeed re collaborative manufacture came to nought. The aircraft was stored until sometime around 1950 when it was scrapped. It is pictured here at Radlett in 1948.

The ordinary Auster J-1 or J/1 Autocrat was the first civilian product made by the Rearsby company after the war. Many were built from reworked military surplus Taylorcraft Austers or Auster V but others were newly welded in the company's frame jigs. G-AIZU was one of these first registered on January 31st, 1947. It was badly damaged in a mishap at Sleep on December 7th, 1963 but restored on January 4th, 1971. Notice the small vertical tail with static-balanced rudder – a lead weight on a steel arm projecting from the rudder's top. This example also shows the long-range belly fuel-tank which was available as an extra and could carry 13.5 gallons. Many Autocrats were supplied with silencers: this example does not have one, merely plain stubs. In their later lives, a majority of Autocrats were updated with more powerful engines and bigger tails to emerge as J-1N Alphas. *Photograph by Mike Hooks*

Probably the most infamous Auster of them all – and for all the wrong reasons – was G-AGXT. It began life as a J-1 Autocrat operated by the United Services Flying Club, forerunner of the Elstree F/C. Later it was upgraded, as were many Autocrats, to J-1N Alpha status with a larger vertical tail, aerodynamically-balanced rudder and small dorsal fin. But this Auster's claim to fame was that it was the first-ever aircraft to be involved in a murder. On October 4th, 1949, a 44-year-old East End second-hand car-dealer, Stanley 'The Spiv' Setty disappeared with £1,000 in £5 notes. On October 21st, a farmer from Tillingham on the Essex marshes of the Thames Estuary spotted a large bag floating in the shallows. He opened it to find a headless and legless torso. Pathologists identified it as that of Baghdad-born Sulman Seti, who had Anglicised his name to Stanley Setty. And the body had been dropped from a great height. Police began interrogating flying clubs and ultimately homed in on one Brian Donald Hume, born in 1918, who had hired G-AGXT on that fateful day. A local taxi driver recalled he had been paid from a large roll of fivers. Hume was then seen loading some heavy packages aboard the Autocrat he had just hired. Setty's head was never found. Hume was arrested and tried, all the while protesting his innocence and claiming he was hired to dump sacks full of forged petrol coupons. Despite the police having found traces of blood all over his flat, those pre-DNA days inevitably led to the jury being undecided. Instead he was found guilty of being an accessory to murder and sent down for 12 years. Released in 1958, and aware he could not be tried for the same crime twice, Hume penned an article for a Sunday tabloid headlined 'I Killed Setty and Got Away with Murder!'. Hume was not finished, though, and a habit of crime took him to Switzerland where he was found guilty of another murder. Extradited and sent to Broadmoor, he was found dead in a field in April 1988. It was said that if you shoved 'GXT's stick forward, Setty's head would rumble up the fuselage and grimace at you from behind the seat! Of course, it was nonsense. In the way of things, Hume lasted longer than the poor Auster which was written off on June 7th, 1969, when attempting to land at Bickmarsh in Worcestershire after the engine failed.

The Slingsby Motor Tutor was a development of the Tutor glider airframe with a conventional undercarriage and the installation of an Aeronca JAP J.99 engine. The goal was to make an aircraft suitable for solo training so that once a student pilot had reached a degree of proficiency he could build up his hours to qualify for a licence economically by flying the solo Motor Tutor. The Ministry of Civil Aviation would not sanction this so the aircraft faded from the scene. Three were built, two by Slingsby Sailplanes Ltd at Kirkbymoorside. Prototype G-AKEY later G-26-1, pictured here and first flown in June, 1948, and G-AKJD which enjoyed a long life before crashing while giving a demonstration at Dunstable Down on June 21st, 1964, when a wing-tip hit the hillside. The third amateur-built aircraft came much later: G-AZSD registered April 7th, 1972.

The de Havilland DH.82a came into its own during the war as a training aircraft. That so many survived to become the mainstay of post-war flying clubs and the 'poor man's Spitfire' of today's private-owner aircraft desire is not surprising. The first big order was placed by the Air Ministry in 1939 and this was for 2,000 machines. While the early examples were built by DH at Hatfield, the majority was by the Rootes Group, which was the overall name for Morris Motors. A relatively large number of these were for Commonwealth use, in particular the RAAF and the RNZAF and many went to the bottom of the sea through enemy torpedo attack on their cargo ships. One example that can be traced from this group was T7187 which saw service with the Royal Navy as a floatplane. This was distinct from those Moths built with floats and operated as DH.82 Queen Bee remotely-controlled aircraft. These all had flat-sided wooden fuselages.

The Tiger Moth was also made in Canada but due to the extreme shortage of Gipsy Majors they were equipped with Menasco D-4 Super Pirate inline inverted 4-cylinder engines. With 125 hp compared to the 130 hp of the original UK engines, the Menasco motors, made in Burbank, California, were slightly heavier at 311 lbs compared with the Gipsy Major's 300 lbs. This tended to give the Canadian-built versions a marginally shorter nose and a decidedly bluff, angular profile with a flat top cowl line. Because the propeller rotation was the opposite direction to the UK original, the nose cowl air vent was on the other side. The Canadian versions also had cockpit canopies to cater for the colder climate while longer exhaust pipes dispensed with the British Tiger's exhaust stubs. It was styled the DH.82C and here is an example, 4861, in profile.

Norman Jones of the Tiger Club conceived a Tiger Moth modified as a single-seater to fly inverted 'for an extended period' and the first example so altered was G-APDZ converted in 1958 and named *The Bishop* in honour of Cyril Albert Nepean Bishop (1901-1968). The second was *The Archbishop* G-ANZZ in 1959 (this one was flown inverted all the way across La Manche from Lympne to Le Touquet on June 27th, 1959). The top wing centre-section fuel tank was dispensed with and replaced by a front cockpit tank while the tailplane carried enlarged elevators and the front end carried a metal propeller. Here we see *The Archbishop*, G-ANZZ (DE974) after an unintentional effort to extend the inverted flying capability to the landing sequence.

De Havilland DH.82a Tiger Moth G-ANUH was an ex-Service machine DE402 which was registered on August 9th, 1954, but was written off in a crash at King's Norton, Birmingham, on June 16th, 1959. Here it displays a useful feature used on most Service training aircraft – the blind-flying hood over the rear cockpit. The pilot is enclosed in a small world inside his canvas cocoon and must fly the aircraft on instruments only. Nobody liked flying under the hood but the consequence was that it certainly served as a quick way of teaching one to fly on the dials! People sometimes ask what the 'a' means in DH.82a. This is the addition of the horizontal anti-spin strakes at the fuselage decking end by the tailplane. The plain DH.82 didn't have them.

Tiger Moth owners are a bold bunch. They know that most flyers would give their eye teeth to fly a Tiggie, so they all walk tall and show-off at every opportunity! The Moth Rally at Beaulieu encourages this behaviour and brings out the very worst in these chaps. Here is a snapshot showing nine of them pretending they can all fly in formation… They're not all that bad, really!

Joseph Richard Currie was engineer to the Cinque Ports Aviation company at Lympne when he conceived the little wooden single-seater biplane that became known at the Wot. His first was G-AFCD registered on November 22nd, 1937. It was powered by an American-made E.113C engine from a discarded Aeronca C-3, G-ADZZ. He then built a second airframe, G-AFDS, registered on March 21st, 1938. This shared the same engine as its predecessor, so the two aircraft could not fly at the same time. There were slight differences between the two machines, namely the bracing of the centre-section pylon and the vertical tail. In this posed picture, Joe Currie is supporting some 500 lbs of the tare weight on his back while his assistant at the tail carries about 50 lbs. The central fellow merely supports the starboard wing-tip. After the war, Viv Bellamy at the Hampshire Aeroplane Club hired Currie and encouraged him to revise the Wot. With the aid of John O Isaacs of Southampton and, later, Dr J H B Urmston (trading as Botley Aircraft) plans for the Wot were prepared and sold to amateur constructors. About a dozen were built with a variety of engines including, experimentally, a Rover Gas Turbine making the World's smallest jet plane!

Besides biplane trainers of which the Tiger Moth was by far the most prolific, the Royal Air Force did have some monoplanes, most popular of which was the Miles M.14a Magister, the Service variant of the Miles Hawk Trainer. Here is an air to air shot of P6382, one of a batch of 100 ordered in 1938 and built by Philip & Powis Aircraft Ltd at Woodley, Reading. A number of these were fitted with blind-flying hoods for the rear cockpit but not this one.

Many Miles Magisters survived the war although being all-wood in construction, their often arduous lives took an expensive toll on their airframes. G-AKAT was built as T9738, one of a 1939-vintage batch of 220 machines. It was civilianised and registered on July 2nd 1947 and put in eighteen years of service to its various owners who gave it the name *Skylark*, seen painted on the side in this 1952 photograph. It was withdrawn from service in November 1965. The aircraft is now preserved close to where it was built by the Museum of Berkshire Aviation where it has returned (more or less) to its military markings and 1939 colour scheme – overall yellow with polished aluminium cowls.

Immediately the war ended, there appeared a new British light aircraft. Designed by Richard C Christophorides, the London-born descendant of a Turkish noble family, he had been working on this during the final year of the war with the result that it was finished for first flight by September 1946. The event took place at Heston at the hands of test pilot Rex F Stedman and the aircraft was the four-seat Chrislea Ace. Prototype G-AHLG was ahead of its time in having a tricycle undercarriage, then still a novelty in private aviation. The Ace had unconventional controls. A steering-wheel was mounted on a shaft which protruded from the instrument panel and this controlled ailerons, elevators and rudder. There were no conventional rudder controls.

All seemed well with the little Ace – until the first flight. The aircraft disappeared somewhat unsteadily into the distance while Stedman tried his level best to get it to turn. It appeared the wide glazed 'all-round-vis' passenger cabin effectively blanketed the tail, meaning the rather important rudder. Finally, and no doubt with some relief, he managed to slither the aircraft around in a mixture of full aileron and bursts of throttle. His eventual return to Heston with a rather white face and tale of unconventional method of turning did not escape the notice of the designer.

Almost immediately, G-AHLG appeared sporting a new twin-tail. Stedman bravely went aloft again – and this time expressed himself more or less satisfied with the rudder response. The Ace was not yet out of trouble, though, and the unorthodox control system came in for almost universal condemnation. Parts of this was due to the fact that the control wheel on its shaft had no 'central' position that could be determined other than by trial and error. With a stick, the pilot can see and feel 'centre'. With 'spectacles' on a control column, the centre is equally obvious. The Ace was the odd man out! Eventually, the makers bowed to the inevitable. Foot pedals were installed for the rudder. Even these were not conventional being more like 'harmonium pedals' than a common-or-garden' stirrup. The Ace remained unconventional to the end but those who owned it swore by it. Twenty-eight were built plus for stretcher-carrying Skyjeeps. In 1952, the Chrislea Aircraft company's assets were sold to a new owner who promptly scrapped all part-built aircraft.

Some aircraft have complex histories. This Miles M.17 Monarch is one of them! Built in April 1939, it was registered G-AFRZ to Lord Malcolm Douglas-Hamilton who kept it Heston where, that November, it was impressed as W6463 and used initially by No.13 EFTS. It served several other units before going to Vickers-Armstrong's CRD at Winchester in March 1944. After the war it was restored to a private owner, B G Heron, at Christchurch and given the registration G-AIDE. It was finished in cream and red and is pictured here at Shoreham on August 6th, 1951. It passed to a well-known private pilot, W P Bowles of Pinner who kept it at Elstree. On October 14th, 1982, it regained its original and rightful registration as G-AFRZ and is currently in store awaiting a fresh lease of life.

The Heath Parasol is an American design dating back to 1926 when Ed Heath designed his small single-seat homebuilt for the 'man in the street' to build. He offered a choice of construction forms. The tubular steel framework of the fuselage could be assembled using bolted fishplates or welded, depending on the choice of the builder. Plans were distributed via a popular US d-i-y magazine and many were made over there. In Britain, there is some evidence to suggest that one, unregistered example was made in about 1932 but this is uncorroborated. Robert H Parker of Esher, Surrey, began building one that he registered G-AFZE on August 25th, 1939. Completed post-war and first flown on January 9th, 1949, it was fitted with a 670 cc inverted 'V' Blackburne TomTit engine. Later re-engined with a 32 hp Bristol Cherub III and, later still, with a larger tail having an aerodynamically-balanced rudder, it flew extensively from Luton where, on April 1st, 1966, it was involved in an accident. It is undergoing rebuild.

Another very different take on the Heath Parasol design was this one, G-AJCK built by the South Hants Ultra Light Aero Club of Christchurch led by Roger H Mann and fitted with a 30 hp ABC Scorpion motor. Registered at the end of 1948, it was hopped by George Errington but was not a good flyer until re-engined with an Aeronca JAP J.99. It was based at Luton for a while. It seems to have been a short-lived example, being withdrawn from use by 1953.

After the war, a number of people who could do did their best to achieve an aviating ambition. Richarda Morrow-Tait (1923-1982) was a lady who wanted to be the first woman to fly round the world. On August 18th, 1948, she set off from Cambridge in a Hills-built Percival Proctor IV, G-AJMU, pictured here, with navigator friend Michael Townsend. It was an eventful flight with numerous mishaps and delays culminating in a bad prang at Tok, Alaska, caused by carburettor icing. It was November 11th, 1948. Short of cash and trying to get her mount repaired, Roberta had to let Townsend go home while she stayed behind. Finally, after many trials and tribulations, she had to abandon the Percival, found some Americans who grub-staked her enterprise and bought her a 1942 Vultee Valiant, NX54084. She even persuaded one Jack Ellis to fill the navigator's seat. On August 19th, 1949, she arrived on Croydon's turf. A year and a day and a different aircraft, but she was certainly the first woman round the globe.

There were five variants of the Percival Proctor, itself derived from the successful pre-war Vega Gull. This one, G-ANYC, was Proctor IV built just at the end of the war as RM222 by F Hills & Sons of Manchester. It was owned and operated by Vendair Ltd of Croydon. First registered on January 8th, 1955, the aircraft was finally withdrawn from use at Elstree and broken up. Many Proctors underwent this fate as they were generally if somewhat erroneously considered too big and too 'thirsty' for economic private use.

Built by Miles during the war largely as a private venture and thereby technically illegally, the Messenger was successfully proposed as an Army liaison aircraft, mainly because of its very slow stalling speed. It was also an ideal candidate for when peace descended once more on what everybody hoped would be a private flying paradise. Of course, once the war was ended, few people had any money, but Miles was well-placed with the Messenger. All told about 80 were built including 21 for the RAF, all civilianised. This one, G-AKBO and finished in the standard Miles' colour scheme of cream and crimson, was first registered on September 4th, 1947, and flew with the Yorkshire Aeroplane Club for almost a decade. Flown by Blackburn test pilot Harold Wood, it won the 1954 King's Cup Race at 133 mph. It is pictured here in 2003 at Turweston when it was in sky blue and white livery.

So encouraged was Miles by the success of the Messenger that a twin-engined version was produced – the M.65 Gemini. The last aeroplane to be built in quantity at Woodley, this used the same wing as the Messenger and proved as great a success. Well over a hundred were built with 97 on the UK register. G-AKDJ was registered in August 1947. It belonged to a paper-towel manufacturing company and on January 5th, 1961, it took off from Blackpool but suffered engine-failure on climb-out. The pilot and sole occupant made the best of a bad job and crashed on Blackpool's Bispham Beach. Before salvage could be organised, the rising tide submerged the wreck causing prolonged salt-water damage from which repair was deemed impractical.

When de Havilland Aircraft of Canada Ltd designed a Tiger Moth replacement, it was both the company's first solo design as well as being the first of stressed-skin all-metal construction – the control surfaces were fabric-covered. This was the DHC.1 Chipmunk and two were sent over to Britain for evaluation. The upshot was that it was adopted as the RAF and RAFVR's new ab initio trainer. There were a few minor changes to the Toronto-made original, the most significant being the shifting forward of the undercarriage by two inches and the increase in elevator movement. Here is a picture of one of those two Canadian-built examples, G-AKDN, taken in 1948.

Chipmunks became the mainstay of RAF training for some years until replaced by the Percival Provost and, later, Jet Provost. Here are three in formation at RAF Swinderby. By 1956, however, the first were being pensioned off for sale to flying clubs and civilian pilots. The Air Registration Board called for extensive modification before they could be granted a full C of A and this work was expensive. It required some expensive pioneering work but eventually they began appearing in increasing numbers on the civil register. In all, DH built 1,014 Chipmunks, many for foreign air forces.

The standard 'Chippie' was powered by the 145 hp Gipsy Major 10 Mk. 2. However, in 1966 Viv Bellamy had the idea of using the Chipmunk as a flying test-bed for the Rover TP-90 118 shp gas turbine. The conversion was carried out at Portsmouth Airport by Hants & Sussex Aviation Ltd which took G-ATTS and turned it into a turbo-prop. It participated in the 1968 SBAC Show at Farnborough and went on to accrue more than 100 hours of development flight before it reverted to its original engine and was sold in America. Bellamy, the man behind the Bournemouth Flying Club and Eastleigh Airport, went on to fit the same engine into a Currie Wot biplane and was also the financial backer for the miserably unsuccessful Hampshire Halcyon twin engined tricycle monoplane. He also owned the last airworthy DH.86 (the famous *Belcroute Bay* of Railway Air Services, G-ACZP) in Britain which, unfortunately, he broke in Madrid and abandoned.

The Fairey Primer tale parallels that of the infamous TSR.2 as far as lost opportunities go. Designed by Ernest Oscar Tips at the Belgian sister company of Fairey's, the Primer was a development of the pre-war Tipsy M. A tandem two-seater single-engined, low-wing monoplane, it had a welded steel tube fuselage with wooden formers, stringers and ribs, the whole fabric-covered. The symmetrically tapered wings included split trailing-edge flaps. The first aircraft, test flown as G-6-4 and later as G-ALBL, was powered by a 145 hp Gipsy Major 10. This had been the original Tipsy M, OO-POM, of 1938. However, the Gosselies factory was targetted by Nazi bombers in May 1940 destroying all drawings and jigs for the aircraft. Meanwhile, the aircraft itself had been dismantled and shipped to England just prior to the war. Used as a company hack until September 1941, it was then stored until evaluated at Boscombe Down post-war when it was decreed a good aircraft for training. Afterwards, the aircraft had to be stripped down in order to recreate the lost drawings. Fairey planned to build ten, but only two were made, one with a Cirrus Major 3 engine. Registrations G-AKSX and G-ALEW were reserved but not taken up. Tested against the Chipmunk, the latter was chosen, the Primer was scrapped, both 'production' models were unfinished, and G-ALBL, seen here at Farnborough in 1950, was dismantled in 1951.

A good picture for a pub quiz and one which must surely earn for its solver a pint of the best. It goes back to the end of the war and to an Army Specification for a two/three-seat high-wing air observation post. The Scottish Aviation Pioneer was one of the successful developments from this, but this particular aircraft was a loser. Auster Aircraft at Rearsby in Leicestershire produced two unusual Auster variants – the Auster Model M and the Model N to A.2/45. The former had the 160 hp Gipsy Major 31 but with this motor it was rather underpowered so the airframe was fitted with a 240 hp Gipsy Queen 34 and this became the Auster N, VL522. Four were allocated but only two built, this and VL523. Slots and flaps abounded, but the aircraft were slightly tail-heavy.

Another for the head-scratching! In the late 1950s research was being undertaken into the subject of boundary-layer control by suction. In 1960 Cambridge University obtained Ministry of Aviation funding to pursue this project by means of a flying testbed. An aircraft was also made available, this being Taylorcraft Auster VF665, originally built as an AOP.6, before being converted to the prototype T.7. It went to Marshalls of Cambridge where it was transformed into the experimental high-lift aircraft known as the Marshall MA.4 to specification ER.184D. For this purpose a revised wing, stronger undercarriage and enlarged fin and rudder were fitted together with a small gas turbine, which drew air through a matrix of 20,000 perforations in the wings, flaps and ailerons. Each ¼-inch diameter hole had a rubber flap-valve. Lift was greatly improved and the MA.4 flew from 1960. It underwent a number of changes including, as pictured here, a fully-faired undercarriage and an anti-spin parachute mounted between the tailwheel and rudder bottom. The stall came at 30 mph. On March 8th, 1966, while engaged in further trials from Teversham, Cambridge, control was lost at 3,500ft and the aircraft entered a dive from which it did not recover. It struck the ground inverted four miles from West Wratting, Suffolk, killing both pilot and observer. No cause for the crash was released, but is thought that a trailing static tube, in the process of being hauled in, became entangled with the tail unit.

Avions Fairey at Gosselies was Fairey Aviation's Belgian subsidiary under the stewardship of ace designer Ernest Oscar Tips. The Tipsy Junior was his first effort after the war. An all-wood single seater, the fuselage was constructed around a wooden girder that was wider than it was deep, the overall shape being created by formers and stringers. Two were built, OO-TIT, described as a Mk.2 with a 62 hp Walter Mikron 2 inline inverted four-cylinder engine, and OO-ULA, described as a Mk.1 with a London-made Aeronca JAP J.99 flat twin. Each aircraft was similar except for the wing-tips. OO-TIT being faired and OO-ULA with a NACA formula tip. OO-TIT, pictured here, flew for the first time on June 30th, 1947, and was displayed at the Brussels Aero Exhibition staged in July 1947. It came to Britain and flew in its Belgian markings for some while but was badly damaged in a hard landing sometime in 1953.

The Mark 1 Tipsy Junior was OO-ULA and this was powered by the little Aeronca engine made in London by J A Prestwick. The present writer flew this one extensively at Elstree, where both Juniors visited from their home base at White Waltham. A very easy aircraft to fly, it was also one of the fastest to be powered by the Aeronca engine, capable of almost 100 mph.

In 1952, OO-ULA was re-engined with a 62 hp Walter Mikron 2 like its sister and at the same time registered to Fairey as G-AMVP. From then on it remained here in England. On July 24th, 1957, Peter Twiss (1921-2011), the first British pilot to fly at more than 1,000 mph, successfully landed the little Tipsy on the aircraft carrier HMS Ark Royal. For part of its time it had a cockpit canopy. Rebuilt after a long time in storage following a heavy landing at Sandown in 1993, it flew again late in 2006 but suffered a further minor landing accident in 2008.

Some aircraft are born unlucky, the outcome of a union between specification and designer that was never quite right from the start. A fair case in point is the sad tale of the Short SB.6 Seamew. After Short Brothers shut its Rochester works and concentrated itself as Short Brothers & Harland Ltd in Belfast, its managing director Dennis Edward Wiseman, appointed Rear Admiral Matthew Slattery as his director responsible for projects and development. Under his guidance, David Keith-Lucas was encouraged to design a lightweight anti-submarine aircraft to replace the Royal Navy Fleet Air Arm's Grumman AS 4s. It had to operate unassisted from carriers in all but the worst of conditions, especially escort carriers of which we still had considerable numbers from the war. The first Seamew flew on August 23rd 1953. Unlike its rival, Fairey's Gannet, it was a single-engined aircraft with one 1,590 shp Armstrong Siddeley Mamba turboprop. Meanwhile defence requirements were, as ever, changing. Despite folding wings, the absence of deck-landing hook made the Seamew operationally unpopular. Aerodynamic shortcomings and handling problems were never fully sorted out and there were several test-flight crashes. Forty-one aircraft were ordered in February 1955. In the end, this was cut right back, but once production had started it was like stopping a goods train – a long process. In the end, some 20 aircraft did 90 minutes of test-flying at Belfast (Sydenham), a 90 minute ferry-flight to Lossiemouth – and there they were broken up for scrap.

Helicopters are not generally as popular as fixed-wing aeroplanes or autogiros but those of the burgeoning days in Britain often had interesting lives. Take G-ALEG, pictured here. This Westland Sikorsky S-51 Mk.1A was the second of the first batch of 149 similar aircraft built at Yeovil under licence to the American designer. It differed from the US original in being powered by a 540 hp Alvis Leonides 521/1 radial engine. It was thought helicopters made good crop-sprayers for agricultural aviation (they were far more expensive that converted Tiger Moths or later dedicated ag-planes) and so Fisons Airwork acquired several for its subsidiary Pest Control Ltd. First flown on December 19th, 1948, it ended up with the Ministry of Supply by 1951. In the interim it had a novel adventure. The next S-51 off the Westland production line was G-ALEI and this was in Switzerland where it was involved in taking care of an invasion of cockchafers in the Canton Valais. On May 1st, 1950, a bad landing meant it was necessary to change its tail boom. The replacement came from the first Fison machine, G-ALEG. With this, G-ALEI carried on flying just three days later. The reprieve was short-lived for the very next afternoon G-ALEI struck a telephone wire and was destroyed in Switzerland's first-ever helicopter crash. Meanwhile, G-ALEG got a new back end from Yeovil.

Some aircraft have devout followers who will not harken to a bad word about their revered machine. Thus it is with caution that I introduce you to the Fairey Rotodyne for there are those who accord it a reverence normally associated with the TSR.2 and the Avro Arrow. Powered by a pair of 2,800 shp Napier Eland N.El.7 turboprops, the Rotodyne was a large hybrid rotorcraft or a compound gyroplane intended, among other things, as a city-centre to airport bus service or, in other words, providing coach-like travel from place to place without need of an airfield. By far the largest transport helicopter of its day, it could seat between 40 and 50 passengers while a freight compartment could carry vehicles. For take-off and landing, the rotor was driven by tip-jets. Each engine supplied air for a pair of opposite rotors; the compressed air was mixed with fuel and burned. As a torqueless rotor system, no anti-torque correction system was required, though propeller pitch was controlled by the rudder pedals for low-speed yaw control. The propellers provided thrust for translational flight while the rotor autorotated. The cockpit controls included a cyclic and collective pitch lever, as in a conventional helicopter. From vertical take-off the Gyrodyne could change to an ordinary aircraft for level flight. The first flight was on November 6th, 1957 and the first successful transition (gyroplane – aircraft – gyroplane) was on April 10th, 1958. Unfortunately those that stood a couple of miles distant from the sole example made, XE521, could hear it running up. Closer still and conversation was of the shouting nature. Truth was that the Rotodyne was so noisy it would never have been allowed near a populace area, let alone a city centre. Everybody had wanted a Rotodyne and Fairey took many orders. All evaporated on noise concerns. XE521 was scrapped.

Under rotorcraft pioneer Raoul Hafner, Bristol Aeroplane Company moved into helicopters in 1946, flying its single-rotor Type 171 the following July. More elegant than its successful Yeovil rivals, the company was never as successful with its designs. One of its projects was the Type 173, the first of which was G-ALBN seen here in BEA livery making its maiden flight on January 3rd, 1952. It underwent Naval trials as XF785 but was never to go into production. A 13-passenger craft, power came from two 850 hp Leonides Major air-cooled 14-cylinder radial engines. In all five were built, the type providing development for the Belvedere cargo helicopter of which 26 were built.

The Planet Satellite was the 'white elephant' of 1948. Designed by Major J N Dundas Heenan, it was a futuristic looking four-seater built of magnesium alloy and with a tail-mounted pusher propeller driven by a 250 hp DH Gipsy Queen 31 mounted amidships. It also had the butterfly tail and a retractable tricycle undercarriage, the nosewheel folding back into a reinforced keel that ran the length of the underside of the fuselage. Financing for the Satellite was unusual with a partnership established with the Distillers Company Ltd while the Planet Aircraft Company operated as a subsidiary of a liquor company. Built in the Robinson Redwing factory at Croydon in 1947, the prototype was taken to Redhill in 1948. It appeared at the SBAC Show at Farnborough in September 1948 and received the registration G-ALOI in April 1949. RAE Farnborough's chief test pilot was Group Captain Hugh J Wilson who, after several long runs down the runway, managed to get the Satellite airborne at Blackbushe. This first flight ended with the collapse of the undercarriage. After repairs, the aircraft was once more flown and, after reaching an altitude of some 20 feet, was gently landed. Even so, the main keel had been cracked by the force of the touch-down. The conclusion of the Air Registration Board was that the aircraft was badly under-stressed and would necessitate a complete redesign. The fuselage of a second example was used in the equally unsuccessful Firth Helicopter, built in 1952 at Thame. Investment in the Planet Satellite topped £100,000 but it was quietly forgotten. G-ALOI gathered dust at Redhill until 1958 when it was broken up.

In 1951 the Popular Flying Association issued a request for a design of a light aeroplane that would be suited to amateur construction. Since the Association had just purchased a large stock of redundant brand new engines from the London-maker J A Prestwich which had been produced in 1937 for the Aeronautical Corporation of Great Britain at Peterborough for its Aeronca 100 aircraft, it was also stipulated than the design should preferably use the Aeronca JAP J.99 engine. Two former DH Technical College students, Forester John Richard Britten (1928-1977) and Nigel Desmond Norman (1929-2002), then making crop-spraying conversions for Tiger Moths, accepted the challenge and designed the BN-1F, G-ALZE. This all-wood aircraft had a cantilever box-structure undercarriage and was unusual, for so small an aircraft, in having flaps. Its first flight at Bembridge on May 16th, 1951, revealed a lack of directional control and insufficient power. Pilot Norman attempted to correct drift but was unsuccessful, the aircraft landing in the close-by Bembridge marshes and tearing off the undercarriage which broke the fuselage completely in two. A new fuselage and conventional braced landing gear was built and the engine replaced by a 55 hp Lycoming for the next trial. Directional control and insufficient lift from the 23 foot span wing generated a raft of changes. First a dorsal fin was fitted and a much-enlarged rudder. Then the span was increased by five feet. Finally finlets were added above and below the tailplane. Further trials established the truth in the saying that if it doesn't work first time, regardless of how much money is thrown at it, it won't improve. In the end, the Luton Minor was selected for the PFA's first all-British home-built design.

Our Royal Family has always been an air-minded lot, even if, in recent times, they find it fashionable to be known for going aloft in helicopters. The controversial King Edward VIII flew from Windsor Castle's one-time Royal airstrip known as Smith's Lawn before he was crowned and the Duke of Edinburgh actually flew solo (as naturally befits the one who sits in a single-seater) in a Rollason Turbulent G-APNZ in 1960 – the first and only single-seat aircraft to have been flown by a member of the Royal family. Less well-known is the fact that Prince Charles harboured a long-standing urge to fly a Tiger Moth. On July 30th, 1979 he went aloft in G-ADIA. Here he is in a classic pose for anyone who has just Tigervated – all grins and cheerfulness!

After the war it seemed logical, to some, that BOAC would want to re-introduce its flying-boat services around the world and so Saunders-Roe at Cowes on the Isle of Wight went ahead and produced the large luxury Princess 200-seater powered by ten 3,780 ehp Bristol Proteus 600 engines in six nacelles, the outer nacelles having one motor while the others had two. Indeed, BOAC ordered three in 1946. By the time they were ready for flight in 1952, plans had changed and the airline no longer planned to use waterplanes as landplanes became larger and more reliable. Geoffrey Tyson got the prototype, G-ALUN, into the air that August 22nd. It was spectacular and beautiful to behold – but nobody wanted it. G-ALUO and G-ALUP were finished, less engines, and towed to Calshot where they were cocooned in foam plastic until 1957 when all three were broken up. Here we see G-ALUN, left, and the unfinished G-ALUO on the Saro slipway on the River Medina with the equally unwanted SA.1 jet-propelled flying-boat fighter – the first of its kind in the world – between them.

The post-war years were the hey-days of the British film industry and aviation films were all the rage. The outcome was that it brought together experts in aviation to act as advisers to the movie producers who went more and more for authenticity. The popular film *Those Magnificent Men and their Flying Machines* demanded the building of flying replicas of contemporary early aircraft. One of these was the Eardley-Billing Biplane, the only record of which was an old and faded photograph. The present author (in shirtsleeves) and Harold Best-Devereux, then chairman of the Popular Flying Association were asked to take on this project. Working at Stapleford Tawney in Essex we built this A-65 Continental-powered concoction with dummy cylinder heads to make it look like an improbable V-8. We both flew it and each measured speeds against a car and confirmed some impossible figures – take-off 30 mph, cruising speed 28 mph. Don't ask how... The film was great fun to make.

When the Royal Air Force sought a replacement for the Chipmunk as a trainer, Percival Aircraft Ltd was in a good position to offer some hardware. Working with them as designer was Polish-Australian Henryk Kazimierz Millicer (1915-1996), better known as Henry Millicer who would go on to distinguish himself 'down-under' with the Victa Airtourer. Back in the 1950s, however, it was Millicer at Luton who came up with the design for a low-wing monoplane with a fixed, tailwheel undercarriage

and side-by-side seating to Air Ministry specification T.16/48. Called the Percival P.56 Provost and powered by an Armstrong Siddeley Cheetah engine, it first flew on February 24th, 1950. Subsequent aircraft would be powered by the 550 hp Alvis Leonides 126 nine-cylinder radial. It proved to be an outstanding trainer and forerunner of the Jet Provost, the RAF's first ab initio jet trainer. Provosts were a great success and served in many parts of the world. In all, 461 were made and at least five ended up on the civil market. G-AMZM, formerly G-23-4, was registered in May 1953 but was sold to the Royal Malaysian Air Force on April 27th, 1961, becoming FM1036.

The first aircraft to be designed, built and produced by Scottish Aviation Ltd at Prestwick was the Pioneer, a design by Robert McIntyre in response to Air Ministry Specification A.4/45 for a light communication aircraft. The prototype was a three-seat high-wing cabin monoplane powered by a 240 hp de Havilland Gipsy Queen. Four prototypes were ordered: in the event, only two were completed and these were marked VL515 and VL516. The first was premiered at the SBAC Show staged at Radlett in September 1947. With the Gipsy Queen, the Pioneer was underpowered and, as a machine with extensive flaps and slots, power was needed to obtain optimum performance. Here Queen-engined VL515 flies in the hands of test pilot Noel J Capper. The performance was judged disappointing. *Picture by Mark Amor*

The prototype Pioneer became the Mk.II. Now fitted with a 520 hp Alvis Leonides nine-cylinder radial engine, first prototype VL515 became XE512, pixtured here. In the interim, VL515 had a short civil career as G-AKBF, first flown on May 5th, 1950. The aircraft demonstrated excellent STOL performance, and was soon being ordered by the RAF. Now known as the Pioneer CC.1, production examples of them were equipped with full-span controlled leading-edge slats and large-area Fowler-type trailing edge flaps, giving a take-off run of 225 feet and a landing run of just 200 feet. The first Pioneer CC.1 to be delivered to the RAF, on August 11th, 1953, was 'ex-prototype' XE512.

A brilliant idea, a radical design and novel construction methods all pulled together to produce the Somers-Kendall SK-1, G-AOBG. Designed by Hugh Kendall, financed by racing pilot Nat Somers and built by Shawcraft (Models) Ltd of Uxbridge, the SK-1 was an all-wood tandem two-seater mid-wing cantilever monoplane with a V-tail and powered by a Turboméca Palas turbojet mounted above the mid-fuselage. The undercarriage comprised a pneumatically-retractable nose wheel and single fixed main wheel, balance being maintained on the ground by means of retracting wing-tip outriggers. The cockpit was enclosed by a one-piece blown canopy. The choice of a laminar-flow wing required extreme accuracy of build-quality so special routing techniques were employed to ensure the perfect profile. Constructed at Woodley between 1954 and 1955, the aircraft was first flown by Nat Somers on October 8th, 1955. Maximum speed at sea-level was 323 mph against a design estimate of 330 mph. It subsequently made an attempt at the 100 km closed-circuit speed record for its class but was frustrated by landing gear problems. Plans for production in a new factory already built at Panshanger Aerodrome were abandoned. The aircraft was retired and stored following an engine failure prior to take-off on July 11th, 1957. *Picture by Mike Hooks*

In the mid-1950s, Sqdn.Ldr James Edward Doran-Webb, who ran the Wiltshire School of Flying, considered that the DH Tiger Moth represented an under-utilisation of resources as it had the potential to carry more than two people. He pointed out that the Fox Moth probably had more drag but, on virtually the same power could fly a pilot and four passengers. The Tiger Moth ought to be able to do similar! So was born the four-seat DH.82a, properly known as the Thruxton Jackaroo – Thruxton for the name of Wiltshire's aerodrome, and Jackaroo for the name given to a young man who is a trainee on an Australian cattle station. With a widened fuselage, centre section and undercarriage, this was a low-cost conversion, the majority of fuselage frames being unaltered. Ronald Prizeman's design gained some popularity after G-AOEX first flew in March 1957. Some 19 Tigers were Jackaroo'ed over the following years including one quite nice one by Rollasons at Croydon but in the end most reverted to normal Moths. The nine-day wonder had time-expired! There are supposed to be half a dozen still in existence including one in Canada. G-AOEX still flies as a Jackaroo with a UK museum..

Earlier we saw a picture of Joseph Richard Currie's little biplane the Currie Wot. Through dint of persuasion, Viv Bellamy of the Hampshire Aeroplane Club at Eastleigh persuaded Joe Curry to revise his design. The outcome was Bellamy's G-APNT and many others built under the auspices of the Popular Flying Association. Gone, though, was the era of the low-powered engines of old and Wots were fitted with engines ranging from VW conversions through Lycomings to, in one experimental case, a Rover gas turbine. R W Hart of Three Bridges in Sussex set about building this one, G-AYNA, in 1970. It was fitted with a 65 hp Continental flat-four. *Picture by Richard Riding*

G-AJCP was a registration allocated to an Avro Anson 1 but it was never taken up. When Group Captain John Christopher Paul, editor of *Air Pictorial* magazine and soon to be a PFA and Royal Aero Club senior executive, got Rollason Aircraft to build him a D.31 Turbulent with a special-category C of A, he successfully applied for this out-of-sequence reg to personalise his aeroplane in March 1959. He kept it at Fairoaks where it stayed, with its next owner, until August 1965 when it changed hands and went to Panshanger. In 1971 he successfully fitted a sliding bubble canopy to blend the existing large windscreen into the aft fuselage.

Norman Herbert Jones, owner of Rollasons at Croydon, had a fixation with the letter 'Z' which is why when he began mass-production of the Druine Turbulent he sweet-talked his way around the registration department of the Ministry of Civil Aviation and reserved every registration ending with a 'Z'. Other than Group Capt Paul's aircraft seen in the previous picture, itself a special registration, all Rollason Turbulents had these distinctive markings. G-APZZ was built in March 1960. On July 10th, 1964, owner and Tiger Club member Robin d'Erlanger was flying back to Biggin Hill from Berck-sur-Mer when he experienced engine failure and he had to ditch in the Channel. Fortunately the Norwegian tanker *Gunmar Brovick* was close by and was able to rescue not only him, but also his Turbulent. Unfortunately it was subsequently discovered that the salt-water immersion, even though short-lived, had damaged the airframe beyond economic repair and the aircraft had to be scrapped.

The Tipsy Nipper was a bold attempt by the Belgian designer E O Tips to make a modern ultralight for home-building. The outcome of this endeavour was rather an ungainly-looking machine where the pilot sat in a cramped cockpit positioned between the two wing spars. Power came from a Stark Stamo, an Ardem or converted VW engine. Aside from home-built examples, there were numbers of Nipper Mk.II machines imported from Belgium (G-ARBP was one of them) while some were built by Slingsby Sailplanes Ltd and by a small business called Nipper Aircraft Ltd. The example here was originally 1,400 cc Stamo-powered but in November 1967 it was re-engined with a 1,834 cc VW. One design issue with the Nipper was its relatively high centre of gravity which, combined with the spindly, small-wheeled undercarriage, made forced landings a little tricky. This one had such an event on June 4th, 1989 when the nose leg broke and the aircraft promptly inverted, trapping the pilot. This was neither the first nor the last such occurrence.

Something different! This is Vickers 618 Viking, G-AJPH, seconded to the Ministry of Supply for use as a flying test-bed for the Rolls-Royce Nene turbojet engine and allocated the markings VX856. It was thus the world's first jet airliner. On July 25th, 1948, the 39th anniversary of Blériot's crossing of the English Channel, the Nene-Viking flew from Heathrow to Villacoublay in the morning carrying letters to Bleriot's widow who met it at the airport. The flight of 222 miles took just 34 minutes. VX850 then flew back to London in the afternoon reaching a maximum speed of 415 mph at 12,000 feet and averaging 394 mph. The Nene was one of the first Whittle-inspired centrifugal compressor engines and was a wholly-new design which emerged as the most powerful motor of its time. The third engine to enter production at Derby, it was built in record time, design to first run being under six months. Sadly it was not to achieve great success, being passed over in favour of the axial-flow Avon that followed it. Its only widespread use in the UK was in the Hawker Sea Hawk and the Supermarine Attacker. In America it was built under licence as the Pratt & Whitney J42 and it powered the Grumman F9F Panther. In a political move I am sure we lived to regret, we gave the technology to the Soviets who used it to power the well-known MiG-15 fighter aircraft which was built in huge numbers. As for VX850, in 1954 it was sold by the MoS and underwent the substantial conversion to Hercules 634 piston engines by Eagle Aviation to join their fleet. It then went trooping as XJ804 before being broken up at Blackbushe in September 1962.

The Newbury AP.4 EoN was designed by Carl Robert Chronander, best remembered for his part in the design of the General Aircraft Cygnet pre-war. Built by Elliotts of Newbury (hence EoN) to the design of Chronander's company, Aviation & Engineering Projects Ltd of Feltham, the four-seat all-wood low-wing monoplane was intended as a multi-purpose machine. Company chief was Horace Caleb George Buckingham (1915-1965) whose firm of furniture-makers had been seconded during the war to make gliders. Now the EoN capitalised on all those finely-honed wartime skills. First flown at Welford on August 8th, 1947, it was found to be under-powered with its 100 hp Cirrus Minor. Upgraded as the EoN II with a 145 hp Gipsy Major 10 and a longer nosewheel strut, it was a success wherever it went. Only problem was the market, a-swim with cheap ex-Service lightplanes and short on cash. On April 14th, 1950, G-AKBC was destroyed in a pilotless take-off through prop-swinging without chocks. It was the final straw in a brave attempt to build a fine aircraft and, with the illness and premature death of the managing director Horace Buckingham, Elliotts' soiree into powered aircraft came to an end. Here it is seen at the SBAC Show, Radlett, in 1947.

When Auster Aircraft Ltd was absorbed into Beagle in 1960, its first products were re-vamped existing designs. Auster had purchased a large number of former Army Auster aircraft during the late 1950s. These were AOP.6, T.7 and T.10 aircraft which were updated and re-engined with the Gipsy Major 10-1-1. Initially two versions were offered for sale on the civilian market from 1960. These were the Auster 6A Tugmaster for utility and glider towing, and the 6B three-seat De Luxe aircraft. When the company became part of Beagle Aircraft in 1960, the Auster 6B was renamed the Terrier. The first of these became the Beagle A.61 Terrier I. In 1962 the Terrier 2 was introduced with a greater span tailplane, wheel spats and a metal propeller. G-ASAK seen here was once a T.7, WE591. Spruced up and given a new paint scheme, it was now promoted as a Beagle Auster A.61 Terrier 2 first registered on June 26th, 1962.

It turned out that the Beagle Terrier was not an economic success for more man-hours were spent on rebuilding each ex-military aircraft than were spent in building the new aircraft for the Army. It was also out-dated as, by 1961, most competing manufacturers were introducing designs which were all-metal. The tricycle undercarriage was now in favour and more modern engines such as Lycoming or Continental from American makers were gaining in popularity. Terriers did enjoy some popularity as a private-owner machine. In all, 18 Terrier 1 aircraft were converted at Rearsby plus 45 Terrier 2. G-ASOM, one-time AOP.6 VF505, was one of the first conversions to Terrier 2 and flew first as G-35-11. On January 8th, 1978, it was flying circuits at St Merryn, Cornwall, when a heavy landing saw it 'written off' as 'damaged beyond repair'. Proving that Austers, like, cats, have more than one life, it was later rebuilt and re-registered on April 19th, 1983, as G-JETS. However, when sold again on August 13th, 1991, the new owner restored the former registration G-ASOM. Few other aircraft have enjoyed so many identities.

Before leaving the world of Terriers, it is worth illustrating the sole example of a Beagle Terrier 3, G-AVYK. The one-time WJ357, an AOP.8, this was the same as a Terrier 2 except for the engine which was a Lycoming O-320, the same as used in the Auster J-5V. This was also the last aircraft to emerge from Rearsby when production ceased there in 1966. Incomplete, it was finished off by engineering apprentices at BEA. Used for glider-towing – note the hook above the tailwheel – there was also the addition of a large dorsal fin which was a legacy of its Army role. By now, it was patently obvious that the world required aircraft with tricycle undercarriages. The rather coarse American slang term 'tail-dragger' was retrospectively applied to many aircraft over here by a largely insensitive tranche of neophyte flyers who had no time to master the skills of a three-point landing. And Beagle knew it must acknowledge the trend. The next from the Auster mould would be an updated variant on a 1957 design – the nose-wheeled Atlantic G-APHT. It would be another dog-inspired flyer, this time the Airedale.

Auster aircraft, even after the Beagle absorption, were nothing if not derivative and the Airedale was no exception. A four-seater with fabric-covered welded steel tube fuselage, it had originally appeared as the Auster D.8 which was in turn a modified tricycle version of the Auster D.6. The Airedale had many similarities to the earlier Auster C.6 Atlantic design of 1957-58 and the first three D.8 airframes were in construction when Beagle Aircraft acquired the company in 1960. Once under the Beagle belt, Beagle began introducing a series of major alterations to the D.8, which included moving the pilot's door aft and adding a second door on the right while widening the rear cabin, lengthening the rear fuselage and adding a swept fin together with many detail changes. Once the prototype, G-ARKE, had undertaken its first flight, a batch of pre-production aircraft followed and detail changes continued. No two aircraft were exactly the same. This emerged as Beagle's design philosophy. As changes continued, these aircraft were repeatedly modified and rebuilt as both weight and costs spiralled. As it was, the performance of the Airedale, although faster than the D.6 on the same engine, was decidedly lacklustre, largely due to its comparatively high structural weight, and it was quite unable to compete in the market with its US competitors. Airedale production ceased in 1963 after just 43 aircraft. It was calculated that the break-even manufacture/production figure could be 675 aircraft – a quite impossible target. As it was, the Airedale took some 6,900 man-hours and £2,037 in labour charges to build, against a selling price below £5,000. At one point in 1963, Beagle had 20 unsold Airedales. Both Airedale and Terrier were seen as stop-gaps whilst more modern aircraft were designed, but each had incurred significant losses, in the case of the Airedale almost £500,000. It appears that a decision in 1962 to continue production past the first 25 aircraft was only made due to the optimistic outlook and predictions of Beagle's rather maverick chairman, Peter Masefield.

As the availability of low cost ex-Service aircraft began to dry up and new aircraft became more expensive, the home-built aircraft movement become more organised and consolidated after its re-establishment under the auspices of the Ultra Light Aircraft Association (1946) which became the Popular Flying Association and today is known as The Light Aircraft Association. The Luton Minor was the last pre-war design for amateur construction and it was taken over by Phoenix Aircraft Limited under whose auspices it was redesigned to meet post-war standards as the Luton LA.4a Minor. Here, however, is a pre-war aircraft, a LA.4 built in 1958-60 at Lake, Sandown, Isle of Wight. Curiously, while this aircraft clearly shows the pre-war style of finless rudder, tail-skid and undercarriage, it has been erroneously described as a LA.4a! G-ASAA has a London-made Aeronca JAP J.99 engine.

Unlike the previous picture, this is a genuine Luton LA.4a Minor with Piper Cub-style undercarriage, tailwheel and fixed fin mounting a round-topped rudder. G-AXGR was first registered in June of 1969. Like the Luton LA.4 in the earlier image, this aircraft is powered by the J A Prestwick-built J.99 copy of the original Aeronca E.113C flat twin engine.

The pre-war Luton LA-5 Major tandem two-seater G-AFMU has already been illustrated. In 1956 this popular pre-war design underwent revision as the Luton LA-6 Major by Phoenix Aircraft. A number were built in Britain and several in Germany and Switzerland. G-AVXG had the misfortune to strike trees while taking off from a farm at Trafford on February 19th, 1976 and was damaged beyond repair while the owner-pilot sadly lost his life. This example had a non-standard fin.

In 1939, L Ron Miller of Beer near Seaton in Devon began building a Luton LA.4 Minor rom the instructions in the monthly magazine *Practical Mechanics*. He completed the airframe and fitted it with an Aeronca JAP J.99 engine. Registered G-AGEP it was ready for flight when the war intervened. Stored carefully throughout the war years it survived to re-emerge in 1946. By this time, Miller had not fared so well and found himself unable to proceed. The Minor changed hands several times before ending up in the hands of George W 'Jack' Gowland. Anxious to fly it, Gowland was also keen that his small son should be able to accompany him to air-displays. So was born the Gowland Jenny Wren. A wholly-new fuselage incorporated a small seat to carry up to 50 lbs weight behind the pilot. Built at Brookmans Park in Hertfordshire, the aircraft was assembled at Panshanger for its first flight on September 2nd 1966. The engine was a 55 hp Lycoming O-145-A2. It used the wings, struts and tail of G-AGEP. A true 1½-seater, it flew successfully for some years until the young Gowland outgrew his small seat.

The Beagle B.121 Pup was an all-metal aerobatic machine created by Beagle Aircraft Ltd at Shoreham Airport. Designed as a two or four-seat touring aircraft, the prototype, G-AVDF (farthest from the camera) made its maiden flight on April 8th, 1967. Shortly afterwards, a more powerful variant appeared. This was the Pup 150 first flown that October as G-AVLM (nearest the camera) with enlarged rudder. First user of the Pup was the Shoreham Flying School in April 1968. There were three variants of the Pup: the Series 1 (100 hp Rolls-Royce Continental O-200A); the Series 2 (150 hp Lycoming O-320-A2B); and the Series 3 (160 hp Lycoming O-320-D2C). The aircraft proved popular and was sold to flying clubs and private users worldwide. The first signs of Beagle's poor management and lack of profitability came when the firm applied for a government loan. In December 1969 the government withdrew its financial support for the business and the company was placed in receivership. Over 250 Pups were on order but production ceased with the 152nd aircraft. Some remaining nearly completed aircraft were finished at a variety of locations but the Shoreham plant closed for good. A military version of the Pup was developed. This was the Beagle B.125 Bulldog with a 200 hp Lycoming engine. Only one prototype aircraft was built by Beagle (with another largely complete) before it ceased operations; the design and production was subsequently taken over by Scottish Aviation.

At the heart of Beagle's business problems was a company policy of continually designing and altering new aircraft which drew drastically on whatever profits were possible in the Beagle Pup. The B.206 seven-seat twin-engined liaison and communication aircraft built is a good case in point. The design began in 1960 and the prototype, G-ARRM, seen here, first flew on August 15th 1961. Designated a B.206X, one this one was made. This was a five-seat all metal low-wing monoplane powered by two Continental flat-six engines. The second prototype, designated a B.206Y, was slightly larger with a larger-span wing and seating for seven. Two aircraft, now called the B.206Z, were built for

evaluation by the Ministry of Aviation at Boscombe Down and an order for twenty aircraft, now changed to B.206R, for the Royal Air Force followed. The RAF examples were known as Basset CC.1 and were built at Rearsby, Leicestershire. There was a Series 1, then a Series 2. And so it went on. Build quantities were in single figures except for the Series 1 (11) and Series 2 (45). A good aircraft hampered by an indecision of management.

The Britten-Norman BN-2 Islander is arguably this country's most successful small airliner. Indeed, from tiny beginnings in the small hangar at Bembridge on the Isle of Wight, the company has seen production of its Islander aircraft top 1,280 examples. Many a company would give their eye teeth to get a fifth of that in terms of marketing success. The twin-engined Islander was a clear-cut case of falling and landing firmly on one's feet because there was simply nothing wrong with it. As an aircraft it was perfect from the moment its piston engines started up for the first time. Prototype G-ATCT was powered by a pair of Continental 1O-360-A engines but production machines, besides having a four-foot greater wing-span, would have a variety of other, bigger engines including models with turboprops. The aircraft pictured here was first flown on June 13th, 1965, and six days later starred at the Paris Air Show. On August 20th, 1966, a second prototype made its first flight. These prototype aircraft, were equipped with less powerful engines. By April 24th, 1967 the first production Islander first flew and type certification followed that August. America certified the type in December 1967

The Britten-Norman Islander entered production on the Isle of Wight and later licensed manufacture to a Romanian company as well. But the Britten-Norman company entered financial difficulties during the late 1960s and was taken over first by Fairey Aviation as Fairey Britten-Norman. This was a short-lived move for Fairey itself then encountered financial problems, resulting in the Fairey Britten-Norman company entering receivership and the firm's subsequent acquisition by Oerlikon Buerle of Switzerland, leading to the formation of Pilatus Britten-Norman, at which point some production activity was transferred back to Bembridge. In 1977, a standard BN-2 was re-engined with Dowty Rotol ducted fans. Some strengthening of the main spar at the root end was required to allow for the extra weight but the outcome was a far quieter power source that produced less noise than conventional propeller propulsion. Eighteen months of flying trials to evaluate the use of the ducted fan as a means of reducing aircraft noise followed: the results showed a 20 db noise reduction as well as increased thrust and reduced pollution. The project was dropped on cost grounds. In 1978, a further improved version, the BN-2B Islander II, was produced as a result of a product improvement programme. The BN-2B model involved several changes, including a redesigned cockpit and a reduction in cabin noise levels. In 1980, it was decided to make available turboprop engines for the type, adopting twin Allison 250-B17C engines; with the latter installed, the aircraft is designated the BN-2T Turbine Islander. The first such BN-2T entered service in 1981.

Britten-Norman was good at doing things in secret behind closed doors. Starting with the BN-1F and proceeding up through the unsuccessful Nymph lightplane, the company had always relied on surprise. Such it was in September 1970 when the Bembridge doors rolled back to reveal a super-stretched Islander with, of all things, a third engine grafted into the tail. This was the prototype Islander Mk.2, properly known as the Trislander. Converted from a standard BN-2, G-ATWU, the 18-seater Mk.3 model first flew on September 11th, 1970, and then went straight to the Farnborough SBAC Show that afternoon. The success of the tiny Bembridge-based company which had begun life in the confines of the former Labour Committee Rooms in Star Street, Ryde, in the early 1950s was meteoric. The bankruptcies and reformations along the way were almost inconsequential. By 1974, sales of the Islander surpassed the 548-order record for all British multi-engine commercial aircraft. In 1982, another production milestone was reached with the delivery of the 1,000th Islander. After the early 1980s, sales began to fall off due to the global market having become saturated. The longevity of the Islander also acted against its own replacement market. In 2016, Britten-Norman claimed that the Islander was in daily service with roughly 500 operators in more than 120 countries.

G-BDTS is described as a Fairey Britten-Norman Mk,III-2 Trislander first registered on March 16th, 1976 and sold to Australia in July, 1978 as VH-EGU. The B-N success story has really been the exact opposite of the remainder of the British aircraft industry. While we no longer have any of the gig names that dominated the first 80 years of aviation in Britain, B-N has gone from strength to strength – via a deal of turbulence along the way. Sadly the founders are both dead now, but their name lives on in the Britten-Norman Group. In February 1999, this was able to announce in had successfully acquired Romaero, the Romanian manufacturer of the Islander, By May 2006, a greater sales emphasis was being placed upon the military version of the Islander called the Defender. In December 2006, *Flight International* observed that: 'The only civil aircraft that remains in production in the UK is the tiny Britten-Norman Islander'. In May 2010, Britten-Norman announced that, due to the rising costs of production in Romania, manufacturing of the Islander would be recalled to a new site in the UK.

The Lockspeiser Land Development Aircraft was the aerial 'pick-up truck' of the late 1960s and all through the years of its promotion it appeared to offer untold advantages which nobody wanted to take up on. Designer David Lockspeiser (1928-2014) envisaged an aircraft that would be capable of transporting anything from cattle to fencing, furniture to engineering equipment. It could also be used for fire-fighting. And, because of the modular design of the aircraft, it would be able to transport its own replacement wings, tail and engine to enable establishment of a 'forward-base'-type of operation. A self-loading ability combined with a four-wheeled 'leg at each corner' undercarriage enabled it to load cargo unaided by taxiing over its cargo, straddling it, and then employing an internal electric winch to raise cargo. A 70% scale model of the LDA (with conventional tricycle undercarriage) was built at Dunsfold and registered G-AVOR, flying in August 1971. Power came from a pusher-mounted 160 hp Lycoming. Promotional development in 1986 saw the aircraft re-registered G-UTIL and renamed the LDA-1000 Boxer. The project was dealt a severe blow in January 1987 when an arson attack on its Old Sarum hangar destroyed it. With the subsequent death of the designer, the project also died.

Racing small aircraft has been a long-standing feature of American private flying since the 1930s. Now styled Formula One Air Racing, it has encouraged the design and construction of small, aerodynamically-derived and powerfully-engined single-seaters. The Owl Racer was the idea of one George Owl of North Carolina in 1969. The prototype was built by John Alford while a second example, registered G-AYMS and named Ricochet, was built by Bill Bowker of Farm Aviation in Hertfordshire and was first flown at Panshanger by Sqdn Ldr Manx A Kelly on April 13th, 1971. The aircraft was raced at North Weald Airfield on the following May 31st but, on the flight back to base (Redhill) later that day, a propeller failure caused it to crash into the River Thames at Greenwich Reach killing the pilot, P T Gent-Eggett. A short-lived and attractive aircraft, it is pictured here at Redhill.

John F Taylor of Ilford, Essex, designed the Taylor JT1 Monoplane at his home in the 1950s. It was in his upstairs flat that the prototype, G-APRT, was built. Aimed at the novice builder, Taylor's aircraft could be built in small domestic spaces with the minimum of basic tools and was intended for low-power engines. The prototype was equipped with a modified J.99 JAP flat twin but later examples were powered by VW conversions such as the Ardem 4CO2. It made its first flight at White Waltham on July 4th, 1959, at the hands of W/Cmdr O V Holmes. At that time it was one of the very earliest brand new designs to be available for the British homebuilder under the auspices of the Popular Flying Association. Weighing just 660 lbs, the 15-feet long monoplane enthused many builders including C J Lodge who built G-AYSH art Broomfield, Chelmsford, which first flew at Tolleshunt d'Arcy on June 19th, 1973.

The Bearn Minicab was a French design from the pen of Yves Gardan in the immediate post-war years. In 1963 the present writer obtained the rights to this design after the builders ceased manufacture at their base in Pau. Re-designed to British design standards as the Ord-Hume GY-201 Minicab with a 90 hp Continental engine, it was approved by the PFA in Britain, the EAA in America and the ULAAofA in Australia. Many examples were built around the world while original factory-built examples became thin on the ground. G-BCLM was a 65 hp French-built model, formerly F-BGSZ. This one crashed at Hurst Farm, Winchfield, Hampshire on September 10th, 1983.

One of the strangest aircraft to be seen in post-war skies was the Edgley EA-7 Optica, a low-speed observation vehicle intended as a low-cost alternative to helicopters. It was powered by a Lycoming flat-six engine situated behind the bubble cabin and driving a fixed pitch ducted fan. Designer John Edgley, at that time a post-graduate student at London's Imperial College of Science & Technology, began the final aerodynamic design in 1974 and a model was wind-tunnel tested in 1975. A company was formed called Edgley Aircraft Ltd which designed and built the prototype. In 1982, investors bought into the project and a production line was set up at Old Sarum Airfield in Wiltshire. Short of an electric engine, Optica was thought to be the world's quietest powered aircraft. Over the next three years the aircraft received UK certification and the first customer aircraft was delivered. Despite this success, the investment necessary for full production did not materialise and the business went into receivership and John Edgley was forced out. With new owners, aircraft on the production line were completed and Optica entered service. A total of 22 aircraft have been manufactured, and construction of a 23rd begun but not completed. Ten aircraft were destroyed in an arson attack at the factory. Several more ownership changes and false starts took place culminating in a new outfit, grandly titled Interflight Global, being formed to re-launch Optica. We wait with breath suitably bated.

There's a strong connection between Great Britain, the Australian all-metal light low-wing Victa Airtourer, seen here, and the Percival Provost – and it's Polish! This little aircraft was the winning design in a competition organised by the Royal Aero Club in 1953. It was submitted by Henry Millicer, the chief aerodynamicist of Australia's Government Aircraft Factories. And it was Polish-born Millicer who once worked at Luton Airport for Percival Aircraft/Hunting Aircraft Ltd. And he was the man behind the Provost. A wooden prototype was constructed by a small group of enthusiasts (the Air Tourer Group of the Australian Ultra Light Aircraft Association) in Melbourne during the late 1950s and first flown on March 31st 1959. After trial flights development continued to the all-metal version. Interest was shown in the design by Victa Ltd, which at that time was best known for making lawn mowers and light two-stroke engines. During the period 1961 to 1966, Victa undertook production of the all-metal Airtourer, building both 100 hp and 115 hp models. Production continued until 1966. All rights to the Airtourer were purchased in 1968 by Aero Engine Services Ltd (AESL) in New Zealand where further production of 115 hp and 150 hp models took place until 1973. AESL pilot Cliff Tait used an Airtourer, ZK-CXU Miss Jacy, for a record breaking flight, circumnavigating the globe between May and August 1969 and covering 53,097 km in 288 flying hours. Miss Jacy is now on display at the MOTAT museum in Auckland. Several Airtourers were exported to Britain and are still flying. Here is one from New Zealand – ZK-CHD.

A rather large fellow in a blazer and harbouring a fairly wide moustache, saw one of these microlights flying overhead. He looked up and said in a loud voice: 'You wouldn't get me up in one of those dam-fool toys!' A close-by chap overheard this and responded: 'At least he is in the air, flying like a bird, while you, sir, stand there with both feet more or less on the ground!' The one in the moustache turned on his verbal assailant. 'You may be right, but one does has self-respect!' There seemed no answer to that, so the close-by chap distanced himself with a shrug. The point was that anything that flies is better than nothing that flies. Put another way, beggars may not be choosers. My only comment would be that any flying machine that calls itself a Mainair Gemini Flash (G-MNNI is said to be one of these) might be suffering a nasty verbal complaint…

Index

Key: OFC = Outside Front Cover   IFC = Inside Front Cover
IBC = Inside Back Cover   OBC = Outside Back Cover

A
A&AEE Martlesham Heath 8, 53, 61, 72, 97,
ABC Hornet 75 hp engine 28; Scorpion 35 hp engine 2, 47, 71, 115
Aberdeen Flying School 42
Acton aerodrome 4
ADC Airdisco 120 hp V8 engine 17; Cirrus 95 hp engine 33
Aer Lingus 62
Aero Engine Services Ltd (AESL) 140
Aeronautical Corporation of America, Inc 84; Aeronca C-3 84, 85; differences from UK-built model 84
Aeronautical Corporation of Great Britain Ltd 84, 85, 124; Aeronca 100 84, 85, 86, 124; Aeronca 300 85
Aeronca E.107 26 hp engine 56; E.113C 37 hp engine 73, 83, 84, 111, 133; Czech copy of 83
Aeronca JAP J.99 37 hp engine 81, 83, 84, 85, 108, 115, 120, 121, 124, 132, 133, 134, 138
Aeroplane, The, magazine 20, 35, 51, 78
Air bridge for airline passengers, the first 94
Air Couriers 67
Air Ministry 109, 126; inspector of accidents 77; specification 87, 91, 99, 103, 126; offered Fane F1/40 102, 103; acquires Monospar ST-25s 104; Small Commercial Aeroplane Competition 8, 12
Air Pictorial magazine 128
Air Registration Board (ARB) 118, 123
Air Taxis Ltd, de Havilland sister company 9, 26, 28
Air Tourer Group of the Australian ULAA 140
Air Training Corps (ATC) 41; Squadron 51
Air Union, operator 16
Airco DH.6 7, 50; DH.9B 11
Aircraft Accessories Ltd 85
Aircraft carrier, Tipsy lands on 121
Aircraft collision with tram 16
Aircraft Exchange & Mart Ltd, Hanworth 85
Aircraft landing one on top of another, frequency of 7
Aircraft, first production with retractable u/c 57
Airship, R33 10; R100 10; R101 10
Airspeed Ltd 107; factory at York 57; AS.5 Courier 46, 49, 57; AS.6/6A Envoy Srs 1/Srs II 49, 57; first production aircraft with retractable u/c 57; AS.8 Viceroy 57; AS.40 Oxford 57; AS.65 Consul 57; builds SM.1 51
Airwork School, Heston 52
Alclad, Bluebird fuselage covered with 69
Alcock, John, transatlantic pilot 16
Aldergrove aerodrome 22
Aldernam aerodrome (later Elstree, *qv*) 30
Alexander Street garage, Flying Flea 72
Alford, John, aircraft builder 138
Alington, Cyril Geoffrey Marmaduke, test pilot 104

Allison 250-B17C turboprop engine 136
Alvis Leonides 521/1 540 hp engine 122, 126; Leonides Major 850 hp engine 123
American aircraft, 'mechanical prejudice' against 90
Angus Aquila 5
Angus, Arthur Leighton, designer & pilot 35
Ansett Airways Ltd 49
Antique Aircraft Association of Australia 52
Anzani engine 11
Apse Heath aerodrome, Shanklin 32, 43, 98
Apse Manor Farm 98
Apsley, Lord, private owner 51
Ardem 1,834cc engine 129, 138
Armitage, Francis W, pilot 24
Armstrong Siddeley Cheetah V engine 46; Cheetah IX 350 hp engine 20, 21; Genet 1 50 hp engine 19; Genet 60 hp engine 22; Genet IIA 80 hp engine 28, 43, 51; Genet Major 105 hp engine 23, 33, 34, 50; Jaguar engine IFC; Lynx IVC engine 57; Lynx VIA 140 hp engine 28; Lynx VII 240 hp engine 20, 21; Mamba 1,590 shp turboprop 136; Mongoose 150 hp engine 100
Armstrong Whitworth Argosy IFC; AW.15 Atalanta 45
Arpin, Morris B, aircraft designer 93, 94; Arpin AR-1 93, 94
Atkin, Keith Leonard, Moth passenger 25
Atlantic, first flight across 16
Auster Aircraft Ltd 107, 119, 130; Atlantic 131, 132; J-1 Autocrat 107, 108; story of a notorious murder involving 108; J-1N Alpha 107, 108; 6A Tugmaster 130; 6B De Luxe 130; D.8 132
Austin Motor Co, aircraft 13; Kestrel 13
Austin, Herbert 13
Australian Aerial Services Ltd 13
Australian Aero Club, Victoria 47
Austro-Daimler 90 hp engine 5; 120 hp engine 6
Autogiro 71, 122; Cierva's 48; confused with helicopter 59; first with shaft-driven rotor 48
Ava 4a.00 27 hp flat-four engine 76, 81
Avery, Philip de Walden 54
Aviation & Engineering Projects Ltd 130
Aviators' Finance Co, Ltd, The 4
Avions Fairey, Gosselies, Belgium 120
Avro 504K 4; replacement for 100; 594 Avian III 19, 21; 616 Sports Avian 33, 34, 43; 619 Five 25, 50; 638 Club Cadet 52; 652A Anson 105; Mk.I 92, 128; Arrow 122; Type 620 23; 685 York 2

B
BA Swallow 36, 49, 55, 70; Mk.2 closed cabin 70
BAC Drone 68, 69
Bage, Arthur, aircraft designer 37, 58, 74
Baginton aerodrome 33, 83
Baldonnel aerodrome, Dublin 62

Balfour, Lionel, aircraft designer 106
Barber, Horatio 5
Barker, Edward Robert, pilot-owner 99
Barnwell, Frank, aircraft designer 15
Barton-in-the-Clay aerodrome 21, 67, 91
Baynes, Leslie, aircraft designer 90
BE.2C shoots down Zeppelin 102
Beagle Aircraft Ltd 130, 132, 135; Beagle A.61 Terrier 130, 131; Terrier 3 131; A.109 Airedale 131, 132; B.121 Pup 134, 135; B.125 Bulldog 134; B.206 135; Basset CC.1 135
Beardmore Aviation test pilot 72, 160 hp engine 12
Bearn Minicab 139
Beddington aerodrome 14
Belfast (Sydenham) aerodrome 121
Bellamy, Vivian Hampson, aviation engineer & benefactor 111, 118, 128
Bembridge Airport 15, 51, 101, 124, 135
Beneš, Pavel, aircraft designer 106
Beneš-Mráz Be-501 Bibi 106
Bennett, Miss Philippa, charter operator 80
Bentley Motors Ltd 31
Berkshire Aviation museum 112
Best-Devereux, Harold, ARB inspector & PFA chairman 125
Bickers, Brian, Air-Britain photographer 97
Bickerton, John Myles, aerodrome owner 31, 64; crash in Chilton 82
'Big Moth, The', nickname 44
Biggin Hill aerodrome 128
Bilborough, Sqdn Ldr H R, Chilton pilot 82
Bishop, Cyril Albert Nepean, pilot 110
Bishop, The, name of Tiger Moth single-seat racer 110
BK Swallow 73
Blackburn Aeroplane & Motor Co Ltd 35; B-2 trainer 69; Beverley, transports DH.51 44; Bluebird 19, 29, 69; Kangaroo 9; test pilot Harold Wood 116; Cirrus engine IFC, 22; Cirrus Minor 1 90 hp engine 70, 74, 79, 80, 93, 130; Cirrus Major 155 hp engine 106, 119; Cirrus-Hermes 105 hp engine 26, 33, 42, 43; 68; Cirrus Hermes II 115 hp engine 32, 34
Blackburne TomTit 670cc engine 114; Thrush 1,090cc engine 22
Blackpool & West Coast Air Services Ltd 61, 62
Blériot's Channel crossing anniversary 129
Blind-flying hood 110, 112
Bootle, founder The Spartan Flying Group 48
Boscombe Down 119, 135
Boulton & Paul hangar 98
Bound, Rowland Henry, designer 24, 37, 58
Boundary layer control experiments 120
Bournemouth Flying Club 118
Bowker, W S 'Bill', Farm Aviation owner 138

Bowles, Walter P, racing pilot 65, 114
Bradbrooke, Francis Delaforce, *Aeroplane's* test-pilot 78
Bramhill, Geoffrey, pilot of Kitten 81
Bristol Aeroplane Company 123; Bristol 89A Trainer 21; Belvedere 123; Berkeley 15; Cherub III 36 hp engine 76, 114; Jupiter Fighter 21; Jupiter IUV engine 21; Jupiter XFBM 595 hp engine 55; Proteus 600 3,780 ehp engine 125; Type 171 123; Type 173 123
Bristol & Wessex Aero Club 51
British Air Racing Champion, 1954 64
British Aircraft BA Swallow 36, 49, 55, 70
British Airways Ltd 41, 60
British Colonial Airways, Croydon 60
British European Airways (BEA) 123; its DH.89A aircraft 105; apprentices finish Auster 131
British Overseas Airways Corporation (BOAC) 125; resume flying-boat services? 125
Britten, Forester John Richard, aircraft designer 124
Britten-Norman Ltd 124; Britten-Norman Group 137; BN-1F 124; BN-2 Islander 135, 136; BN-2 Defender 137; Mk.3 Trislander 136, 137; BN-2T Turbine Islander 136
Broad, Hubert, test-pilot 90
Brooklands aerodrome 30, 56, 102
Brooklands Museum 69
Brookmans Park, Hertfordshire 134
Brown, Arthur 16
Broxbourne aerodrome 70, 81
Bruce, Robert A, Westland director 19
Bruce, The Hon Mrs Victor, pilot 35, 41
Brussels Aero Exhibition, 1947 120
Buckingham, Master Caleb George, Elliotts' director 130
Bugatti Club 106
Bulman, George, test pilot 100
Burgess, R F, wireless operator 41
Burgoyne, Donovan Cookes, aircraft builder 73
Burgoyne-Stirling Dicer 73
Burnelli, Vincent, his flying wing projects 96
Butser Hill, Petersfield 101
Byrne, Mr & Mrs Ernest, Shanklin Flying Services 98

C
Calshot, flying boats at 125
Cambridge aerodrome 115
Cambridge University 120
Camm, Sydney, aircraft designer 100
Capper, Noel J, test pilot 126
Carden, Sir John Valentine, inventor 69, 90; Carden-Ford 30 hp engine 69, 81, 90, 94; Carden-Baynes Aircraft Ltd 90; Carden-Baynes Bee 90
Cardiff Aeroplane Club 80
Cardington 10
Castle Bromwich aerodrome 49

Central Aircraft Company, Kilburn 11
Central Centaur IIA 12; Centaur IV 11, 12
Chadwick, Mervyn, co-designer 78
Chadwick, Roy, aircraft designer 50
Charles, HRH Prince, flies Tiger Moth 124
Chilton Aircraft Ltd 81, 82; DW.1/DW.1a 81, 82, 94
Chorlton, Michael C, film-director 106
Chrislea Aircraft Co 113; Ace 113; Skyjeep 113
Christchurch aerodrome 114, 115
Christophorides, Richard C, aircraft designer 113
Chronander, Carl Robert, aircraft designer 74, 101, 130
Cierva C.19 autogiro 48; 30; Mk.II 23; C.30/30A 48, 71
Cierva, Juan de la, autogiro designer 17, 48
Cinque Ports Aviation 111; Flying Club IBC
Cirrus Hermes I 105 hp engine - *see under* Blackburn
City & Guilds 96
Clare Valley aerodrome 52
Clear, Ronald Edward, test pilot 4
Cleaver, Lt.Col Arthur Spencer 22
Cleaver, Mrs Franklin Spencer, pilot 22
Clerget 130 hp engine 7
Clive-Smith, H, aircraft owner 106
Clutton, Eric C, aircraft designer IBC; FRED IBC
CLW Aviation Ltd 72; Curlew 72
Cobham Air Routes Ltd 34, 50; sells airline operation to Olley 50
Cobham, Sir Alan, pilot 18, 34, 57
Cockerell, Stanley, test pilot 18
Cole, Stanton Wilding, EKCO radio company 72
College of Aeronautical Engineering, Redhill 43
Colt Automatic gun 5
Commercial Air Hire Ltd, Hon Mrs Victor Bruce's company 41
Comper Aircraft Ltd 1, 66, 83; Fly 102, 103; Kite 53; Mouse 53; Scamp 102, 103; Streak 53, 54; Swift OFC, 1, 4, 47, 102
Comper & Walker Ltd 83
Comper Fane Aircraft Ltd 102
Comper, Flt Lt Nicholas IFC, 47, 53, 54, 83, 102
Continental engine 103, 125, 128, 131; A-65 65 hp engine 103, 125, 128, 131; A-80 80 hp engine 103, 125, 128, 131; C-90 90 hp engine 135; IO-360.A engine 135
Control column, 'came loose in hand' 24
Coombs, Harry Charles, Sandown & Shanklin Flying Services Ltd 32, 98
Cornwall, George, aircraft designer 66
Cosmelli, Charles Henry 'Jack', aircraft owner 101
Cotswold Aero Club 65
Coupé Deutsch Race, Étampes 54
Courtenay, William, author 26
Courtney, Frank T 12
Cowes Airport – *see also* Somerton 98; Spartan factory at 32; Harbour 51

141

Coxon, John Ernest, aircraft owner 101
Cranwell 7
Cricklewood factory, Handley Page's 7
Croskin, Albert Bishop, pilot 25
Cross, Jack, Essex Aero 58
Croydon Airport IFC, 14, 22, 40, 41, 46, 50, 60, 64, 71, 88, 105, 115, 123, 127; aircraft collision with tram 16; record flight by Drone 68
Cull, George, photographer 31
Cullen, G H, Ogilvy's passenger 52
Currie, Joseph Richard, aircraft designer 111, 128, IBC; Wot 111, 118, 128, IBC
Curtiss-Wright Junior 51
CW Aircraft, Ltd, Hanworth 101; bought by General Aircraft Ltd 101; Cygnet 74, 130

D

D'Erlanger, Robin, pilot 128
Daily Express Air Race, Shoreham, 1951 82
Daily Mail Fifty Years of Flying Exhibition, Hendon, 1951 71
Dalrymple, The Hon Andrew William Henry, Chilton designer 81
Darley Monoplane 73
Dart Aircraft Ltd 76, 81; Kitten 81; Pup 76
Davenport, Arthur, aircraft designer 99
David Kay, aircraft inventor 59
Davis, John Henry, aircraft buyer 101
De Havilland Aircraft Ltd, Stag Lane aerodrome 9, 28; DH.51 17, 44; DH.51A 17; DH.51B 17; DH.60 Moth 18, 19, 68; Avian popularity rivals that of 34; DH.60G Gipsy Moth 22, 23, 24, 29, 31, 36; with Cockpit canopy 23; quest for replacement aircraft 59; DH.60G-III Moth Major 58, 68; DH.60X Cirrus Moth 25; DH. 75/75A Hawk Moth, originally named Moth Six 20, 21, 28; DH.80A Puss Moth 30, 31, 32, 36, 42; Puss Moth, Hinkler's death in 24; DH.82a Tiger Moth 3, 47, 68, 69, 109, 110, 112, 127; on floats 109; converted for inverted flight 110; Rootes Group builders 109; DH.82a Tiger Moth, converted for inverted flight 110; DH.82a Tiger Moth, Prince Charles flies in 124; Chipmunk as replacement 117, 119, 126; DH.82B Queen Bee 109; DH.82C Tiger Moth (Canadian-built) 109; DH.83 Fox Moth 46, 51, 127 ; DH.84 Dragon 51, 60, 62; formation flight with Mignet's Pou-du-Ciel 71; Dragon 2 52, 60, 63; DH.86/86A/86B Express 52, 60, 61, 63, 118, IBC, OBC; DH.87 Hornet Moth 59, 91; evolution of DH.87A and DH.87B 59; DH.89 Rapide 52, 60, 62, 63, 105, IBC; original name 'Dragon Six' 62; DH.89A Rapide addition of flaps 62; DH.89B 105; DH.89M Military Rapide 105; DH.90 Dragonfly 52, 63; DH.91 Albatross 87, 88, 89;
DH.92 Dolphin 52, 63; DH.94 Moth Minor 2, 36, 98; DH.106 Comet 18; DH.114 Heron 18; DH.121 (Hawker Siddeley) Trident 18
De Havilland constant speed propellers 88; Ghost engine 20, 21; Gipsy I & II engine 20, 68; Gipsy II 120 hp engine 27, 35, 37; Gipsy III 120 hp first inverted Gipsy 42, 47; Gipsy Minor 90 hp engine 98; Gipsy Major 1 130 hp engine 52, 53, 63; extreme shortage of forces alternative 109; Gipsy Major 145/7 hp high-compression engine 54, 65; 10 Mk.2 118, 119, 130; six-cylinder version becomes Queen 60; Gipsy Six/Queen 200 hp engine 60, 61, 62, 63, 66, 74, 91, 119, 123, 126; Gipsy Twelve 525 hp engine 88
De Havilland Aircraft of Canada Ltd 117; Toronto factory 46; DHC.1 Chipmunk 48, 117, 118, 119
De Havilland Flying School, Stag Lane 11
De Havilland Technical College 18, 81, 94
De Havilland, Capt (later Sir) Geoffrey 22, 36, 60, 91
Denham aerodrome 31, 33, 48, 52, 64, 68, 82, 95, 101
Denman, Lt.Col Roderick P G, pilot 45
Desoutter Company, Croydon 26
Desoutter Mk.I, Hanworth crash 26
Distillers Company Ltd, Planet Satellite backer 123
Dobell, Arthur Edward, pilot 23
Doig, Robert Galloway, Scheldemusch pilot 92
Dolman, Henry James 'Harry', Flea builder 71
Dominie, RAF name for DH Rapide 62
Doran-Webb, Sqdn.Ldr James Edward, aircraft designer 127
Dornier Flugzeugwerke 17
Douglas DC-2 88
Douglas flat twin engine 49; Sprite 23 hp engine 68
Douglas, Fl.Off A C, pilot 41
Douglas-Hamilton, Lord Malcolm, aircraft owner 114
Dovercourt Bay, Kent 92
Dower, Gandar, airline pioneer 43
Dowty retractable undercarriage 66
Dowty Rotol ducted fans fitted to Britten-Norman Islander 136
Dragon Six, de Havilland's original name for Rapide 62
Drew, Capt Donald, pilot 22
Druine D.31 Turbulent 128
Dundas, Laurence Aldred Mervyn, Earl 26
Dundas, R K, aircraft broker 46
Dunlop Aerowheel 31
Dunsfold aerodrome 137
Dunstable 76
Dunstable Dart 76
Dunstable Down, Motor Tutor crash at 108
Dutheil et Chalmers engine 3
Dyce aerodrome 43

E

Eagle Aviation, Ltd 129
Eardley-Billing Biplane replica 124
Eastern Canada Air Lines Ltd 104
Eastleigh Airport 59, 80, 118
East-to-West, first Atlantic crossing by woman 75
Edgley Aircraft Ltd 139; EA-7 Optica 139
Edgley, John, aircraft designer 139
Edinburgh, Duke of, solo flight 124
Egerton, Maurice, aerial photography pioneer 5
EKCO radio company 72
Ellenbrook Club, The 32
Elliotts of Newbury 130
Ellis, Jack, navigator 115
Elstree aerodrome 30, 66, 70, 85, 101, 114, 116, 121; Flying Club 108
England-Australia 1919 air race 13
ENV 35 hp engine 4
Errington, George Bertram Salusbury, test pilot 4, 115
Essex Aero Ltd 58, 72
Experimental Aircraft Association (EAA) 139
Experimental Group, ULAA 94, 106
Experimental Light Aeroplane Club, Nottingham 49

F

Fairey Aviation Ltd 93, 104, 121; acquires Britten-Norman 136; Belgian subsidiary 120; Gannet 121; Primer 119; Rotodyne 122; Swordfish 93
Fairey, Sir Charles Richard 43; his private aerodrome Heath Row 79
Fairoaks aerodrome 74, 99, 128
Fairwood Flying Group 79
Fane Aircraft Ltd 102; F1/40 Air Observation Post 102
Fane Engineering Designs Ltd 103
Fane, Gerard William Reginald, aircraft designer 102
Farman F.61 Goliath 16
Farnborough – *see also under* SBAC) 8, 96, 118
Fifty Years of Flying Exhibition, Hendon, 1951 71
Film industry sponsors replica aircraft 125
Filton aerodrome 101
Findlay, Capt Maxwell Hutcheon 7
Firth Helicopter 123
Fisk, Mr & Mrs Apse Heath airfield 98
Fisons Airwork Ltd 122
Fletcher, Anthony Armstrong 11, 12
Flight International magazine 137
Flower, John Keane, aircraft owner 78
Flugzeugbau Friedrichshafen, GmbH 17
Flying Flea, Henri Mignet's 71, 72, 73, 78, 92, 95
Flying Runabout Experimental Design (FRED) IBC
Fokker F.12 crash 32
Fokker wing technology, used by Avro 50
Folding wings 36
Folkestone Trophy Race 1936 84
Forbes-Sempill, William, F, pilot 25, 68
Ford 4AT-E 2
Ford car engine in Foster Wikner Wicko 79
Formula One Air Racing 138
Foster Wikner Wicko IFC, 79, 80; Warferry IFC, 80
Fraser's Flying School, Kingsbury 13
Fresson, Capt Edward E, pilot 29

G

Gardan, Yves, aircraft designer 139
Gatwick aerodrome 60, 67, 101, 104
Gehlen, Karl, chief of design 17
General Aircraft Company Ltd 74, 101; buys CW Aircraft Ltd 101; Cygnet II 101, 130; GAL.42 Cygnet 101; GAL.47 103; Monospar ST-25 Universal 104; Air Ministry acquires 104
Genet engine – *see under* Armstrong Siddeley
Gent-Eggett, P T, pilot of Owl Racer 138
George, Lloyd, Coalition Liberal Party Prime Minister 23
Gibbs-Smith, Charles, historian 3
Glenny & Henderson Gadfly 56
Gnôme 50 hp engine 6
Goodwin-Castleman, Lt Frederick Benjamin 12
Goodyear Aerowheel 31
Goodyear Trophy, 1957, winner of 65
Gordon Dove 78
Gordon, Raymond, co-designer 78
Gouge, George, aircraft designer 67
Gould, E H, Redwing part-owner 43
Government Aircraft Factory, Australian 140
Gowland, George W 'Jack', aircraft designer/builder 134; Gowland Jenny Wren 134
Grahame-White Aviation Co Ltd 9; Military Biplane 5; Type VII 6; Type X 6
Grahame-White, Claude, aviation pioneer 6, 8
Grainger, Charles Frederick H 50
Granger Archaeopteryx 49
Granger Brothers, aircraft designers & builders 49
Granger, Richard Francis Turney 49
Granger, Richard John Turney 49
Gravesend aerodrome, Kent 72, 74, 92
Great Western aerodrome, Heath Row 43, 79
Great Yarmouth Naval Air Station 6
Green 100 hp engine 6
Green, Alfred Edward, Dart Pup owner 76
Green, Ron, founder The Spartan Flying Group 48
Grey, Charles Grey, founding editor *The Aeroplane* 35
Grieve, John, aircraft inventor 59
Grosvenor Cup Race 82
Grubb, Richard, Aeronca test pilot 84
Grumman AS.4 121
Grumman F9F Panther 129
Guernsey Aero Club 34
Guest, Frederick, The 23
Guest, Rt.Hon Frederick Edward 'Freddie' 23
Guggenheim Institute 96
Guild of Air Pilots & Air Navigators 23
Guinness, The Hon Arthur Ernest 42
Gulf Aviation Ltd 62
Guthrie, Sir Giles Connop McEachern, racing pilot 75

H

Hafner, Raoul, helicopter designer 123
Hagg, Arthur Ernest, aircraft designer 46, 87

Halford, Major Frank, engine designer 20, 60
Hampshire Aeroplane Club 111, 128
Hampshire Halcyon 118
Hamsey Green aerodrome 76
Handasyde, George H, aircraft designer 55
Handley Page Ltd 7, 16, 52; name enters dictionary 7; wing slots 21, 100; HP.42 27, 86; O/400 7, 86; Victor V-bomber 52
Handley Page, Frederick 27, 86; his dislike of bracing wires 27; thoughts on bracing wires *vs.* struts 86
Hanger Lane Farm 4
Hants & Sussex Aviation Ltd 118
Hanworth aerodrome 23, 25, 26, 31, 48, 55, 56, 64, 69, 70, 74, 84, 85, 93, 104; London Air Park Flying Club 84
Harrison's Garage, Loudwater, High Wycombe, Dart Kitten kit 81
Hart, R W, Currie Wot builder 128
Hatfield aerodrome 53, 59, 60, 62, 63, 75, 89, 91, 94, 105; 1938 SBAC Show at 86; RAeC Garden Party at, 1958 24
Hattersley, Patrick Kilvington, Puss Moth owner 32
Hawker Sea Hawk 129; Tomtit 100
Hawker Siddeley HS121 (initially de Havilland) Trident 18
Hawksridge aerodrome 31, 64
Heath Parasol 114, 115
Heath Row (*later* Heathrow), Sir C R Fairey's private aerodrome 43, 79, 95
Heath, Ed, aircraft designer 114
Heathrow-Villacoublay Nene-Viking's record 17
Heenan, Major Dundas J N, aircraft designer 123
Henderson, Basil Balfour, designer 24, 37, 73, 91
Henderson, Col G L P, pilot 56
Hendon aerodrome 71; first SBAC show at 40; 1932 SBAC Show 69; 1934 SBAC Show at 49, 57; German air raid on 75
Hendy Aircraft Co Ltd 24, 37, merges with Parnall 73; 3308 Heck 73
Henly's, car showroom and Autogiro 71
Henshaw, Alex, racing pilot 58, 74
Heron, B B, aircraft owner 114
Heron, J A, engineer 101
Heston aerodrome 38, 39, 43, 52, 53, 54, 64, 66, 71, 83, 90, 94, 103, 113, 114
Heston Aircraft Ltd 1, 53, 66, 102; Phoenix 1, 66
Hill, Capt Geoffrey Terence Roland, tailless aircraft exponent 49
Hillman, Edward, airline founder 51, 62
Hills & Son Ltd, F, aircraft builders 83, 116, builder of Morrow-Tait's Proctor 115
Hillson Praga 83
Hindmarsh, Percy, Vintage Aeroplane Club 68
Hinkler, Herbert J 'Bert', pilot 24; death in Puss Moth 24; Ibis 24
Hirtenberg HS9A 101
Hirtenberger Patronen Zündhutchen und Metallwarenfabrik, AG 101

Hirth HM.60 engine 51
Hispano-Suiza Viper 180 hp engine 8
HMS *Ark Royal*, Tipsy lands on 121
Holder, John Eric Duncan, pilot 64
Holmes, Wing Cmdr O V 'Titch', test pilot 138
Holyman, Victor, Australian airline founder, killed 61
Hoofa, F, Desoutter passenger 26
Hordern, Edmund Gwyn, aircraft designer 55, 66
Horsfield, D, aileron improver 56
Hounslow Heath aerodrome 13, 14
Hucks Starter 8
Hucks, Capt Bentfield Charles, pilot & inventor 8
Hull Aero Club 25
Hume, Brian Donald, case of the air-dropped body 108
'Hungerford Four', Chilton aircraft 83
Hunter Ltd, James, 'hunterised' airfields 43
Hunter, Claude P, pilot 43
Hunterized airfield surfaces 43
Hunting Aircraft Ltd 140
Hurle-Hobbs, Basil Henry St Andrew 64

I
Imperial Airways 18, 22, 25, 27, 33, 45, 55, 60, 61, 62, 86, 88
Imperial College of Science & Technology, London 139
India, partition of 107
Inland Flying Services 98
Instone Air Line 18
Interflight Global 139
Isaacs, John O, aircraft builder 111
Isle of Wight Airport 98

J
JAP 1,000cc engine – see also under J A Prestwich Ltd 93
JEM Aviation, Omaka 47
Jersey Airways Ltd 35
Johannesburg Air Race 7
Johnson, Amy, pilot 31
Johnson, Lt.Col Edward Pardee, Stinson importer 45
Jones, Alan, test-pilot 106
Jones, Norman Herbert, Tiger Club founder & owner of Rollasons 110, 128
Jones, Owen Cathcart, pilot 42
Jowett Cars, Praga B engine-makers 83
Joyce Green aerodrome 16

K
K registrations 10
Kay, David, autogyro inventor 59; Kay Gyroplane 59
Keith-Lucas, David, aircraft designer 121
Kelly, Sqdn.Ldr Manx A. test pilot 138
Kemble aerodrome 46, 57, 73
Kendall, Hugh, racing pilot 127
Kenworthy, John, aircraft designer 13
Kerwin, John Daniel, pilot 26
King Edward VIII, HRH Prince of Wales, future 40, 124
King's Cup Air Race, 1930 25, 32; 1931 31; 1932 69; 1933 83; 1934 42, 53, 54, 59; 91; 1935 65; 1937 75, 80; 1950 78, 79; 1954 116; 1958 65
Kingsbury aerodrome 13
Kingwill, Archibald Norman, pilot 72, 96
Klemm L.25 49; Swallow 70

Knight, Harry, farm-worker killed by low-flying Moth 44
Koolhoven FK-21 26
Kronfeld Ltd 69; Drone de Luxe 69

L
L'Erée private aerodrome, Guernsey 34, 50
Labour Committee Rooms, Ryde 136
Lancing College, Shoreham 4
Lang Propellers Ltd 85
Larkin Aircraft Supply Co 8
Latimer-Needham, Cecil Hugh, aircraft designer 49, 95
Le Bourget aerodrome 41
Le Touquet 110
Lea Farm, Sandown 98
Lea Ltd, S T, aircraft importers 49
Leaf, Miss Freydis, ATA pilot 64
Leicester East aerodrome 68
Levell, Arthur, aircraft designer 72
Lewis, The Hon Brian, pilot 30
Light Aircraft Association (LAA) 83, 132
Light Planes (Lancashire) Ltd 18
Lockheed Constellation inspired by DH.91 89
Lockspeiser, David, aircraft designer 137; Land Development Aircraft 137; LDA-1000 Boxer 137
Lodge, C J, aircraft builder 138
London Air Park Flying Club, Hanworth 84
London Airport, the first 14
Longton, Sqdn.Ldr Walter 19
Lossiemouth RAF aerodrome, Moray 57
Lowdell, George, pilot 49
Lowe-Wylde, Charles Herbert, aircraft designer 68
Low-flying Moth kills farm-worker 44
Lunken Airport, Cincinnati 84
Lusty, James F, company director 79
Lusty's furniture factory 79
Luton aerodrome 115
Luton Aircraft Ltd 49, 95, 132; LA.4 Minor 2, 95, 132, 133; LA.4A 124, 132, 133; LA.5 Major 95, 133
Luton, Percival Aircraft Ltd at 75
Luxmoore, Flt.Lt Francis, aircraft designer 106
Lycoming O-145.A2 55 hp engine 82, 124, 134; O-320-A2B 150 hp engine 131, 134; 160 hp engine 137
Lymne aerodrome 70, 110, 111; Light Aircraft Competitions at 19, 22
Lympne Lightplane Trials 19

M
Machine gun, first aircraft to be fitted with 5
Maclaren, Owen Finlay, castoring wheel inventor 93
MacRobertson Race to Australia 49
Mallik, Suhrid, pilot of Moth 44
Manley, Tom, Bibi passenger 106
Mann, Roger H, aircraft builder 115
Markham, Beryl, pilot 75
Marshalls of Cambridge 120; Marshall MA.4 120
Martin, Bernard, Nottingham-born aviator 15
Martlesham Heath, A&AEE aerodrome 8, 53, 61, 72, 97

Masefield, Peter, Bristol director 132
Master of Sempill, The, pilot 25, 68
Maurice Farman S.7 biplane 6
Maylands aerodrome, Essex 51
McClean, Lt-Col Sir Francis Kennedy 5
McClure, Ivor H, pilot 22
McIntyre, Robert, aircraft designer 126
'Mechanical prejudice' against US aircraft 90
Melrose, Charles James 'Jimmy', racing pilot 66
Menasco Pirate C-4 125 hp engine 96, 109
Merseyside Aero & Sports Ltd 43
MiG-15 fighter jet, British engine 129
Mignet, Henri, amateur pioneer 71, 72; his HM-14 Flying Flea 70, 78, 92
Miles Aircraft Ltd 64; M.2/2A Hawk series 64, 65; Hawk Trainer 112; M.2F Hawk Major 64; M.2M Sparrowhawk 65; M.11a Whitney Straight 65; M.14a Magister 91, 112; 'a gentleman's Miles Magister' 98; M.17 Monarch 65, 114; M.48 Messenger 116, 117; M.65 Gemini 117; Martlet – see also Southern Martlet 27
Miles, Frederick G, aircraft designer 27, 65
Miles, George H, his first aircraft design 65
Miller, L Ron, Luton Minor builder 134
Millicer, Henry, aircraft designer 140
Millicer, Henryk Kazierierz (Henry Millicer), aircraft designer 126
Mills, Bertram, circus proprietor 68; Cyril, Moth Major owner 68
Ministry of Aviation 135; funding for experiments 120
Ministry of Civil Aviation 108, 128
Ministry of Supply 122
Minster Lovell aerodrome (Witney) 97
Mole, Sqdn.Ldr Edward Lucas, pilot 95
Morane-Saulnier fuselage 6
Morris Motors Ltd 109
Morrow-Tait, Richarda, attempts to fly round the world 115
Moss Brothers Aircraft Ltd 78; Mosscraft MA.1/2 78, 79
Moss Ronald L, Moss Aircraft director 78
Moss, Brian P, Moss Aircraft director 78
Moss, Geoffrey P, Moss Aircraft director 78
Moss, Richard A S, Moss Aircraft director 78
Moss, William Henry, Moss Aircraft director 78
MOTAT Museum, Auckland 140
Moth Rally, Beaulieu, The 111
Mráz, Jaroslav, aircraft designer 106
Murray Aeronautical Corporation 84
Murray, Cameron Lathrop Lee, aircraft co-designer 51
Museum of Flight, Scotland's 59
Mynors, Grp.Capt John Travers, pilot 32

N
Napier Eland N.E17 2,800 shp turboprops 122; Rapier 324 hp 'H' engine 57
Napier, Carrill Stanley, pilot 22
Nash & Thompson Ltd 73
National Air Races 82
National Aircraft Factory No.1 14
National Flying Services Ltd, Hanworth 25, 26
National Physical Laboratory 96
Naval Air Station, Great Yarmouth 5
Nazi *Hakenkreuz* 101
New Salts Farm, Shoreham 4
Newbury AP.4 EoN, Elliott's 130
Newham, Charles, pilot 49
Newman, Flt.Lt E H, pilot 53
Newton Heath, Avro factory at 25
Nipper Aircraft Ltd 129
Norman, Nigel Desmond, aircraft designer 124
Norman, Sir Torquil Patrick Alexander 63
North Eastern Airways, Croydon 46
North Weald aerodrome 138
North, John Dudley, aircraft designer 5, 6
Northern & Scottish Airways Ltd 60
Northolt aerodrome 11, 12, 105
Norton Griffiths Trophy 65
Norway, Neville Shute 57
Nuffield, Lord 49

O
Oddie, Bradbury & Cull, rotor makers 59
Oerlikon Buerle of Switzerland acquires Britten-Norman 136
Ogden, Robert William Henry, pilot 50
Ogilvie, Walter Scott, owner-pilot of Kitten 81
Ogilvy, Jock, Handley Page flight test observer 52
Old Sarum aerodrome 139; arson attack on hangar 137
Old Warden aerodrome OFC, 4, 18, 44, 48, 49, 97, 100
Olley Air Services 50, 62; buys Cobham's struggling airline 50
Olley, Hugh Nichol, test-pilot 97
Olympia exhibition centre 5, 8
Olympia sailplane 82
Openshaw, Laurence Pratt, pilot 19
Ord-Hume GY-201 Minicab 139
Owl Racer 138
Owl, George, aircraft designer-builder 138

P
Paine, Ronald Royal, racing pilot 64, 86
Panshanger aerodrome 127, 128, 134, 138
Paris Air Show, 1966 135
Parker, Robert H, aircraft builder 114
Parnall Heck 2C 91; Type 382 91
Paul, Grp.Capt John Christopher, Turbulent owner 128
Pendeford aerodrome 78
Percival Aircraft Ltd, Gravesend 74; at Luton 126, 140; D.6 Gull Six 74; D-Series Gull 74; Mailplane – see under Saro-Percival Mailplane; Mew Gull 58; P.56 Provost 118, 126, 140; Jet Provost 118, 126; Proctor 36, 74, 75, 116; Morrow-Tait's 115; Vega Gull 74, 75, 116

Percival, Edgar IFC, 37, 38, 58, 73, 79
Pest Control Ltd, by helicopter 122
Peterborough Aircraft Ltd 85, 86; Ely 700 86
Peterborough, Aeronca factory at 84
Petter, William Edward Willoughby, aircraft designer 99
Philips & Powis Aircraft (Reading) 22, 65, 112
Phoenix Aircraft Ltd 95, 132, 133
Phoenix Garage 95; fire at 95
Pickering, C L aileron improver 56
Pierson, Rex, aircraft designer 18
Piffard, Harold Hume, aircraft designer 4; Biplane No.2 4
Pilatus Britten-Norman Ltd 136
Pilgrim, Arthur Robert 'Tiny', aircraft owner 66, 85
Piper Cub-style cockpit doors 95; J-2 Cub 99; J-4A Cub Coupé 99
Planet Aircraft Ltd 123; Planet Satellite 123
Pobjoy 75 hp engine 59; 90 hp engine OFC, 1, 49, 51, 67, 70, 72; Niagara 90 hp engine 53, 78
Pobjoy, Douglas Rudolph, engine designer 47
Pollock, Hugh MacDowell, Irish Minister of Finance 22
Pope, Flt.Lt Sydney Leo Gregory, pilot 25
Popular Flying Association (PFA) 79, 124, 125, 128, 132, 138, 139
Porteous, Ranald, test pilot 82, 94
Portsmouth aerodrome 75, 98, 106, 118
Portsmouth Aviation Ltd 106, 107; Aerocar 106, 107; Aerocar Major 106
Portsmouth, Southsea & Isle of Wight Aviation Ltd 41, 46, 57, 98, 106
Pothercary, John, pilot 43
Pou-du-Ciel – see also under Flying Flea 71
Practical Mechanics magazine, aircraft construction articles in 125
Praga (ČKD-Praga) aircraft 83; B2 40 hp engine 92; E.114 Air Baby 83
Pratt & Whitney J42 engine 129
Premier Aircraft Constructions Ltd 78
Prestwich Ltd, J A, engine makers 84, 85, 121, 124, 133
Prestwick Pioneer 99
Prizeman, Ronald, aircraft designer 127
Propeller, DH constant-speed 88
Pugh, Fl.Lt John Bernard Walter, pilot 41
Pulham RAF airship base 10

Q
Queen Mary College, London 96
Queen Mary, ocean liner 57

R
Radlett aerodrome 86, 130
RAF (Royal Aircraft Factory) 1A 90 hp engine 17
RAF Station Great Dunmow 32; Sealand 32
RAF (Royal Air Force) Museum 30
Railway Air Services 60, 61, 118, IBC, OBC
Rand Airport 75
Reading Aero Club 64
Rearsby aerodrome 107, 119, 135

143

Redhill aerodrome 67, 106, 123, 138
Registrations, civil, first 'G-A---' 22; the 'K' numbers 11
Reid, Wilfrid Thomas, aircraft designer 15
Renault 70 hp engine 11
Renfrew aerodrome 60
Riding, Richard, photographer & editor IBC
River Medina, Saro factory on 125
Robinson Redwing 28, 43, 123
Rochester, Short Brothers' factory at 55, 67
Rocky Mountains, flight over 79
Roe & Co, Ltd, A V 23; Hamble 24
Rollason Aircraft Ltd 127, 128; D.31 Turbulent 128; Royal solo flight in 124
Rollason Ltd, W A, Croydon 98
Rolls-Royce Avon turbojet 129; Condor 650 hp engine 15; Continental O-200A 100 hp engine 134; Eagle VIII 360 hp engine 13, 18; Nene turbojet 129
Romaero, Romanian makers of BN-2 137
Roof with German seaplane impaled 17
Rootes Group, Tiger Moth builders 109
Rotor tip-jets 122
Rover TP-90 118 shp gas turbine 111, 118, 128
Royal Academy 4
Royal Aero Club 5, 128; aircraft design competition 140
Royal Aeronautical Society Garden Party, 1937, Heath Row 101; 1939 Heath Row 79, 95, 96
Royal Air Force 112, 126; Pageant, Hendon 30; first ab initio jet trainer 126
Royal Australian Air Force 51
Royal Malaysian Air Force 126
Royal Navy Fleet Air Arm 121; uses Tiger Moth floatplane 109
Royal Naval Air Service (RNAS) 7, 102
Ryan B-1 Brougham 21
Ryde aerodrome 57

S
SABENA airline 50
Sage Ltd, Frederick, Aeronca takes over factory 85
Salmson 75 hp engine 70; AD.9 engine 24, 35, 55
Sandown & Shanklin Flying Services Ltd 32, 98
Sandown aerodrome 98, 121
Saro – see also under Saunders-Roe; A.17 Cutty Sark 35, 40; A.19 Cloud 35; A.21 Windhover 35; Saro-Percival A.24 Mailplane 37, 39; Saro SA.1 jet flying-boat fighter 125
Sassoon, Sir Phillip, pilot 25
Saunders-Roe Ltd (see also Saro) 35, 37, 40, 52, 125; Princess 125; SA.1 jet flying-boat fighter 125
SBAC – see under Society of British Aircraft Constructors; first show at Hendon 40; 1932 Hendon 49, 57, 67; Hatfield 1938 86; Radlett, 1947 106, 107, 126, 130; 1948, Farnborough 123; 1949 106, 107; 1968, Farnborough 118; 1970 136

Schelde Scheldemusch 92
Scheldt Sparrow 92
Schlesinger Race 1936 65, 75
Science Museum Collection 71
Scott Flying Squirrel 25 hp engine 72
Scott, Charles William Anderson, racing pilot 75
Scottish Aircraft Construction Co Ltd 90
Scottish Aviation Ltd 126; Pioneer Mk.I/II 119, 126; takes over Beagle Bulldog manufacture 134
SE.5A 8
Seaplane impaled on roof, German 17
Sempill, The Master of, pilot 25, 68
Seti, Sulman, real name of Setty the 'spiv' 108
Setty, Stanley, 'spiv' car-dealer, notorious Auster murder 108
Shackleton, W S, aircraft brokers 58, 86
Shackleton, William Stancliffe, aircraft designer 51
Shackleton-Murray SM.1 51
Shanklin aerodrome 98; Apse Heath 32, 98
Shanklin Flying Services 98
Shawcraft (Models) Ltd, aircraft builders 127
Shelmerdine, Lady, wife of aviation director-general 104
Sherry E W, aircraft designer 15
Shoreham aerodrome 22, 134; Daily Express Air Race, 1951 82
Shoreham Flying School 134
Short Brothers, Rochester 5, 35; S.16 Scion Mk.I/Mk,II 67; S.17 Kent 55; L.17 landplane 55; S.33, flies through Tower Bridge 5; S.59 5; S.8/1 Calcutta 25
Short Brothers & Harland Ltd 121; SB.6 Seamew 121
Shuttleworth Collection OFC, 4, 18, 100; Trust, The 31, 44, 49
Shuttleworth, Richard Ormonde, pilot 47, 48
Simmonds Spartan 32, 98
Simpson, Paul, Aeronca restorer 84
Simpson, The Rev Frederick A 24
Simpsons Aerospares Ltd, Elstree 32
Skegness Aero Pageant 1932 22
Skinner, Harold William Chetwind 'Bill', test pilot 65
Skyways Avro York 2
Slattery, Rear Admiral Matthew, Short director 121
Slinfold Airstrip, Surrey 43
Slingsby Sailplanes Ltd 108, 129; Motor Tutor 108; Tutor glider 108
Slot, Theodor, aircraft designer 92
Slough Trading Estate 74
Smith, Victor, Schlesinger Race winner 65
Smith's Aircraft Instruments Ltd 75
Smith's Lawn, Royal airstrip 124
Society of British Aircraft Constructors (SBAC) – see also under SBAC; first show at Hendon 40
Soden, F/O Frank Ormond 'Mongoose', pilot 19

Solar Wings Typhoon S/Galley Trike microlight 140
Somers, Nat, racing pilot 127
Somers-Kendall SK-1 127
Somerton aerodrome 37, 52
Sopwith Aircraft Ltd 8; Antelope 8; F.1 Camel 7; Wallaby 8, 13
Sound City Films, dummy airfield builders 44
South Hants Ultra Light Aero Club 115
Southend Airport 72
Southern Aircraft Ltd – see also Miles; Martlet 27
Spafford, Capt John, pilot 18
Spanish Civil War 105
Spartan Air Lines Ltd 37, 41
Spartan Aircraft Ltd 41; Arrow 41, 48; A.24 Mailplane 39; Clipper 52; Cruiser Mk.1 40, 41; Mk.II 41; Mk.III 41; Three-seater 32, 41
Spartan Flying Group, The 48
Spooner, Mrs Winifred, pilot 23
Stack, Thomas Neville, pilot 39
Stag Lane aerodrome 9, 11, 20, 22, 51, 52, 46, 42, 28, 31, 61
Stansted aerodrome 2
Stapleford Tawney aerodrome 125
Stark Stamo 1,400cc engine 129
Stearman-Hammond 'Y' 93
Stedman, Rex F, test pilot 113
Stephen, Major Edward Freer 49
Stieger, Helmuth J, aircraft designer 104
Stinson Junior 45; Reliant 90
Stirling, F/O Frederick Howard, pilot 64, 73
Stisted, H C G, Hinkler Ibis owner 24
Storey, Chris L, Flea builder 72
Straight, Whitney Willard, aviation entrepreneur 73
Strange, Lt.Col Louis Arbon, pilot 40
Stroud & District Technical College 51
Surrey Flying Services 14, 44
Sweeting, founder The Spartan Flying Group 48

T
Tachbrook aerodrome 76
Tait, Cliff, AESL test pilot 140
Tangmere aerodrome 41
Taylor, Cyril W, aircraft co-designer 94
Taylor, John F, aircraft designer-builder 138; JT1 Monoplane 76, 77, 138
Taylor, Richard Harold, aircraft designer 76, 77
Taylorcraft Auster – see also under Auster 107, 120
Taylor-Watkinson Ding-Bat 83, 94
Tempelhof aerodrome 68
Thames Estuary, discovery of human remains dropped from Auster 108
Thornycroft, John Isaac, engineer 4
Those Magnificent Men and their Flying Machines film 125
Thruxton aerodrome 127; Thruxton Jackaroo 127
Tiger Club, The 128
Tiltman, Alfred Hessell, designer 46, 57
Tips, Ernest Oscar, aircraft designer 97, 119, 120, 129

Tipsy B aircraft 97; M 119; S aircraft 78; Trainer 1 97; Junior Mk.I/II 120, 121; lands on aircraft carrier 121
Tipsy Light Aircraft Ltd 97; Nipper 129
Tolleshunt d'Arcy aerodrome 138
Tower Bridge, Short S.33 flies through 5
Townsend, Michael, navigator 115
Train 4T 45 hp engine 81
Tram, Croydon aircraft collision with 16
TSR.2 122; abandoned design 119
Turboméca Palas turbojet 127
Turnhouse aerodrome, Edinburgh 9
Turweston aerodrome, Northamptonshire 116
Twiss, Peter, test pilot 121; lands Tipsy on aircraft carrier 121
Tyson, Geoffrey, test-pilot 125

U
Ultra Light Aircraft Association (ULAA) 94, 106, 132
Ultra Light Aircraft Association of Australia 139
Undercarriage, castoring 93
United Services Flying Club 108
Urmston, Dr J H B, pilot and aircraft builder 111

V
Vendair Ltd, Croydon aircraft brokers 116
Vickers Aircraft Ltd 16; Vimy 16; Commercial 16; Vulcan 18; Wellington bomber 76; 618 Viking fitted with Rolls-Royce Nene turbojets 129
Vickers-Armstrong Ltd 114
Victa Ltd 140; Airtourer 126, 140
Victoria, Queen 3
Vintage Aeroplane Club, Denham 52, 68
Vintage Group, The 33
Volkswagen (VW) 1,800cc converted engine 129; 66 hp engine IBC
Vultee Valiant, Morrow-Tait's 115

W
Waddington, James Ivor, aircraft designer 74, 101
Waddon aerodrome 14
Waight, Robert John, test-pilot 87
Wales, Prince of (future King Edward VIII) 40
Walker, Francis R, Comper co-director 83
Wallis, Sir Barnes Neville, his geodetic structure 76
Walney Island 80
Walter Ltd, A J, Hanworth, importers 99
Walter Mikron 62 hp engine 82, 95, 102, 106, 120, 121
Ward, Alexander Reginald, Chilton designer 81
Warren, James A Crosby, test-pilot 94
Waterhouse, Albert C, BAC Drone owner 68
Watkinson, Eric T, aircraft co-designer 94

Watson, Preston Albert, aircraft designer 3
Watson, Sir Norman J, Comper director 53
Weir Pixie engine 76
Weir, Air Commodore James George 17
Welford aerodrome 130
Welham, Francis, aircraft designer 72
Westland Aircraft Works 8, 73; tailless development work 49; Limousine 8; Lysander, STOL pioneer 99; Sikorsky S-51 122; Wessex 50; IV Wessex 33, 34, 50; Widgeon 19, 22
Westland-Hill Pterodactyl 20
Weston Air Services 55
Wheels, castoring 93
Whitchurch Airport 27
White Waltham aerodrome 33, 106, 121, 138
Whittle, Sir Frank, jet-engine inventor 129
Wicko, Foster Wikner 79; Warferry IFC, 80
Wikner, Geoffrey Neville, aircraft designer IFC, 79
Willoughby Delta Company 96; Delta 8 96
Willoughby, Percival Nesbitt, aircraft designer 96
Wilson, Grp.Capt Hugh J, test pilot 123
Wilson Airways Ltd 50
Wilson Airways Ltd, Nairobi 25
Wilson, Capt Vernon Gorry, pilot 25
Wiltshire School of Flying 99, 127
Wing tips, tapered, Hornet Moth problems with 59, 91
Wingfield, George, solicitor 4
Wing-folding, benefits of 36
Wiseman, Dennis Edward, Short Bros MD 121
Witney & Oxford Aero Club 97
Witney (Minster Lovell) aerodrome, Oxfordshire 81, 97
Wolseley Aries III engine 49
Wolseley Hispano Viper 200 hp engine 8
Wood, Harold, Blackburn test pilot 116
Woodley aerodrome 127; Miles factory at 65, 117
Wright Brothers 3; Wilbur 5
Wright Whirlwind engine 49; J-5 300 hp engine 21
Wroxall aerodrome, Kenilworth 76
Wymeswold, RAF station 73
Wynne-Eyton, George, test-pilot 93

Y
Yapton Aero Club 41
Yate aerodrome 73, 91
Yeovil aerodrome 22
York, Airspeed factory at 57
Yorkshire Aeroplane Club 22, 116

Z
Zander & Weyl Ltd, aircraft builders 76
Zander, Eric, aircraft designer 76
Zeppelin L21, shot down 102
'Zulu-shield' auxiliary fins 61